STAND ready

Ellen Harbin

Scriptures marked NIV are taken from the NEW
INTERNATIONAL VERSION (NIV): Scripture taken from
THE HOLY BIBLE, NEW INTERNATIONAL VERSION ®.
Copyright© 1973, 1978, 1984, 2011 by Biblica, Inc.™.
Used by permission of Zondervan

Scriptures marked KJV are taken from the KING JAMES
VERSION (KJV): KING JAMES VERSION, public domain.

ISBN: 9781695233805

SLOW Livin'
Fraser, MI

ellenharbin.com

DEDICATION

To my children—
Christine (Brandon), Andrew (Taylor),
Eric (Rebecca), Troy (Kaitlin),
Jaylen and Sukanya—
I have no greater joy than knowing you follow Jesus.
As you already know, in life we face things worth fighting for.
It is my hope you will be ready to fight right.
It is my honor and privilege to fight right on your behalf.
It is my prayer you will stand firm in your faith, ready to face
every fight worth fighting for with God's armor secure and
His Word hidden in your heart.
Nehemiah 4:14
3 John 4

STAND ready / Ellen Harbin

CONTENTS

ACKNOWLEDGMENTS

I am forever grateful to those who shared their talent, expertise, and wisdom. Your involvement and support are appreciated.

Dianne Bogdan—editor
Jenny Johnson—cover design
Joe Cummings—author photo
Jerry Cummings—cover photo
The Sequel—writing warriors
Melena Cummings—business advisor
ACCESS prayer team, Christ Church Fraser—prayer support

Kevin—I choose to do life with you.
I chose to fight for us more than fight with you.
We certainly have stood side-by-side through some worthy fights—and I will continue to choose to be ready to fight right for the things worth fighting for.
I am, and always will be, devoted to you.

INTRODUCTION

Welcome to the third book in the STAND series. Over the years of teaching Bible Study, speaking at conferences and retreats, mentoring and discipling, and listening to others share their life stories, I have found one glaring, yet sad reality that rings true: many are not prepared to face hard issues, and they are not ready to fight right for the things worth fighting for.

Waiting until we are engaged in a fight is not the time to figure out a battle plan. We cannot be prepared for a crisis or ready to face a myriad of challenges if we go into them unprepared.

Each chapter of "STAND ready" introduces specific people from the Old Testament books of Judges, 1 and 2 Samuel, and 1 and 2 Kings who were equipped and ready to fight for some relevant matters that are worth fighting for. It is my hope and prayer that you will be encouraged to grow, challenged to change, and influenced to live as Jesus intends—ready to fight right!

Throughout each chapter **KEY POINTS** are intentionally emphasized to encourage you to stand ready. At the end of each chapter, four recurring sections provide opportunity for in-depth personal study or to assist in facilitating group discussion.

PONDER: to deeply, carefully, and thoughtfully consider

PERSUADE: God's Word influences, encourages, and guides

PRACTICAL: applying Biblical Truth to present day

PERSONAL: inviting Jesus into your current reality

Mighty God, thank you for your promises. Your Word is filled with encouragement and assurances of how we face the issues that matter—those things that require we stand ready to fight for. You tell us we can stand firm. You promise that we are not alone. You assure us that Your ways are best. You encourage us with your presence. Thank you for being our strength, our provider, and our hope. Holy Spirit empower and sustain us as we fully rely on you, standing ready to fight right! As we study your Word, transform our minds and revive our hearts.
In Jesus' Name, Amen

STAND ready / Ellen Harbin

1
be ready to fight FAIR

"And what does the Lord require of you?
To act justly and to love mercy and to walk
humbly with your God."
Micah 6:8

"We don't live in a fair house!" I have been a mother for thirty years and have asserted this declaration repeatedly to my six children. My youngest two are now in high school; therefore, the proverbial light at the end of the tunnel is no longer a glimmer. Understanding shines bright as they are now fully aware our family has steadily proven the statement true.

In the Harbin House my husband and I knew early on we would not raise our kids to believe, think, desire, or feel they could apply or invite the aggrandized adjective into our family.

"Hey, that's not fair! Why does *she* get a piece of gum and *I* don't?"

"Honey, you know we don't live in a fair house."

The simple mantra was also relevant in decisive ways, like when a child was trying to plead their case.

"But, that's not fair! He got *his* driver's license at sixteen!"

"Well, son, that's because we don't live in a fair house."

We desired the concept be planted deep, growing roots in their young hearts and minds; therefore, we never tired of declaring and expressing the refrain—*we don't live in a fair house.*

Fair.

When used as an adjective; this word has many separate definitions. My family may not live in a fair house, but we do expect everyone to be fair—honest, just, and genuine, and to follow rules. And because there are things worth fighting for, we want them to fight right. Fighting right, fights fair.

KEY POINT: FIGHTING FAIR IS NOT ABOUT GETTING WHAT WE WANT

The Book of Judges, in the Old Testament, characterizes the Hebrew people, the Israelites, after Moses delivered them from bondage in Egypt and after Joshua led them into the Promised Land, but before the nation was ruled by kings. Twice, the same words are recorded in Judges describing their way of life at that time. Judges 17:6 and 21:25 expresses, "In those days, Israel had no king; everyone did as he saw fit."

By nature we are selfish. The first humans proved this to be true. Eve was selfish in the recorded dialogue with Satan disguised as a snake while Adam paid attention nearby. Genesis 3 tells how her focus turned inward. She saw what she thought would please and satisfy her. Adam and Eve got what they wanted, but it was not what God wanted for them.

It is easy to point a finger at Adam and Eve and talk about their selfishness. *In those days everyone did as they saw fit* could be applied when only two humans dwelled on Earth, and it can also be applied today in our current culture. It seems everyone *wants what they want* and will do *what they want* to get *what they want*.

But let us not look at Adam, Eve, the Israelites, or our current culture. For this moment look at yourself. I am looking at me and you are looking at you. How often are our motives, actions, or thoughts driven by getting what we want?

If we are to fight fair, we need to get our eyes off ourselves and onto the things worth fighting for. If our focus is to do what we think is best, we will fail our friends and families instead of fighting for them.

There are many things worth fighting for—marriage, family, careers, reputation, country, freedom, and safety. And there are many things worth fighting against—addiction, abuse, domestic violence, neglect, hunger, and terrorism. Not exhaustive lists, but things we can agree on. When we trust the bigger picture to God's vantage point, we will fight right. When we have our eyes where they belong, we fight fair.

Do we all stand in agreement on how to fight fair for such things? Well, perhaps the more fitting question is, *can* we stand in agreement on how to fight fair? Since God's Word contains strategies to fight right and fair, for followers of Jesus, the answer is, "Yes, we can!"

But if our motive is to get what we want, we will struggle to fight fair. If our motivation is to fight right and do it God's way, we will fight fair.

Deborah lived during the days in Judges when everyone did as they saw fit. However, Deborah did not care to get her own way; she took care to live God's way as she fought right for the things worth fighting for. Therefore, she fought fair.

In Judges 4:4, we find Deborah's introduction. It says, "Deborah, a prophetess, the wife of Lappidoth, was leading Israel at that time." Before we get to know Deborah, let us take a careful look into the last three words of Judges 4:4.

Whenever we read the three words *at that time* in Scripture, it is helpful to understand them in their context. I appreciate details. Like a puzzle requiring all the pieces to make a complete picture or a detective needing all the evidence to confidently solve a case, I value knowing specific details. These three words, *at that time*, should beg the question, "At *what* time?"

In Genesis God chose to establish a covenant relationship with humanity through one man. If Abraham followed the Lord, listened to the Lord, and obeyed the Lord, God would bless him and make him into a great nation, and all peoples on earth would be blessed through him. (Genesis 12:2-3) Years later Paul, the writer of Romans, says, "Against all hope, Abraham in hope believed and so became the father of many nations, just as it had been said to him..." (Romans 4:18)

God continued his covenant promise through Abraham's bloodline. His grandson, Jacob, who was later called Israel, had twelve sons, and *just as it had been said to him*, Abraham was the start of a great nation. One of Jacob's sons was Joseph. When he was a boy, his older brothers were jealous of him and eventually sold him into slavery, and he landed in Egypt. (Genesis 37-50) God's grace was on Joseph as He preserved the family. He initiated

6

covenant with Joseph through the unfortunate circumstances of his life.

Years later a famine struck the land where Jacob's entire family lived, and through a series of circumstances, they all landed in Egypt. A family was reunited and restored. It is not easy to sum up in a few sentences all that happened *at that time*. But hang on because we are still connecting pieces.

Fast-forward a few hundred years, when we come to the beginning of the book of Exodus. While in Egypt Jacob's twelve sons collectively increased in number and "...the Israelites were fruitful and multiplied greatly and became exceedingly numerous, so that the land was filled with them." (Exodus 1:7) The Egyptian pharaoh feared the increase would lead to his kingdom's demise, so he made them his slaves.

Enter Moses. God raised him up to deliver His people out of bondage and into the Promised Land. Though they marched out of Egypt, they did not enter the land God had provided for them. Instead, they wandered in the wilderness and remained stuck between bondage and freedom. After Moses died Joshua became the leader of the Israelites, and through his leadership, they entered the Promised Land.

And the Israelites began to take possession of the land as the twelve tribes (which began with twelve brothers hundreds of years before) disbursed to their designated locations. After Joshua died Judges 2:10-11 sums up what things were like *at that time*, "After that generation had been gathered to their fathers, another generation grew up, who knew neither the Lord nor what he had done for Israel. Then the Israelites did evil in the eyes of the Lord..."

God continued to protect and provide for His children. But they forsook Him. And it was *at that time*—the time God's people abandoned Him; the time when God's people quit on Him; the time when God's people deserted Him. And it was *at that time* Deborah became one of a few judges to lead Israel.

After grabbing some pieces of the past, it is easier to comprehend and fathom how *In those days, everyone did as they saw fit* became the theme of the day. Before Deborah is named there are three other judges mentioned. The first one led the nation into 40 years of peace, the second into another 80 years of peace, and the third is recognized to have saved Israel. But the years in-between the ruling judges were spent in a downward cycle of mass rebellion and sweeping disobedience.

Judges 4:1-3 explains the oppression Israel was living under. They forsook the Lord, again, and He punished them as He said He would. The Lord sold them into the hands of King Jabin, and for 20 years he cruelly oppressed them.

Wait. God *sold* the Israelites? His chosen people? He *sold* them into the hands of an evil king? That does not seem fair. Ah-ha! There it is—*that's not fair!* Who forsook whom? God doesn't want His children far away, but He's not the one who moved. God is steady. God is faithful. God is immovable—and that includes His statutes and ordinances. He had detailed expectations of how the Israelites were to live, and He gave them clear directives of what would happen if they disobeyed.

KEY POINT: BEING STILL IS READY TO FIGHT FAIR

We cannot be still before the Lord and simultaneously do as we see fit. *Still* has a front-row seat before God. *Still* stays put. *Still* does not waiver or wander. *Still* trusts the Holy One who initiates a covenant relationship.

We cannot begin fighting any battle until we are still. We may need to physically move, but spiritually, we are still. As Moses led the Israelite people—over one million people—out of Egypt, everyone was terrified. They stood at the edge of the Red Sea, hemmed in by the desert, with an army of Egyptian soldiers advancing from behind. But in Exodus 14:14, Moses says, "The Lord will fight for you; you need only to *be still.*" (emphasis mine)

God's people were not still, and it showed. "The Israelites did evil in the eyes of the Lord," is often repeated throughout the Book of Judges. Though hundreds of years have passed, the words of Moses were relevant *at that time* of the judges. And yet, though a nation is predominantly living contrary to God's ways, there is a remnant ready to fight for the right thing.

Deborah is part of that remnant. After 20 years of oppressive cruelty, the Israelites cried out to the Lord for help. And Deborah is God's response to their cry. Her name means *bee.* To her friends she is sweet, but she can be sharp and sting when necessary.

Judges 4:4-5 gives us a few tidbits of information proving this woman is ready to fight for the things worth fighting for.

- She was a **prophetess**. This means she was a mouthpiece for God. When Deborah spoke, when she led, when she judged, God's words came out of her mouth, and they were used for God's purposes.

Her responsibilities in this appointed position included informing, encouraging, and rebuking God's people. Matthew Henry, the commentator, says she was intimately acquainted with God. She would listen to Him, deeply desiring to know His will and communicate it to His people.

- She was a **leader**. It is true not everyone is a leader, per se, but every follower of Jesus should lead well. Moms, dads, husbands, wives, employees, employers, brothers, sisters, friends, neighbors, church-goers—the list is long—insert whatever hat you wear, and you have an opportunity to lead. The question is, do you lead well?

Deborah was leading Israel *at that time*. When most of the nation was living as they saw fit, Deborah was leading. When her fellow Israelites were doing evil in the eyes of the Lord, Deborah was leading. As her people were sold into the hands of a wretched king, she continued to lead. When everyone around her was confused, caught in the snare of chaos, and crying out in despair, Deborah was leading.

Not a passive leading; rather, a ruling, governing, and vindicating style of godly leadership. Deborah was wise, discerning, engaging in controversy for truth's sake, and executing sound judgement, upholding God's statutes and ordinances.

- She **held court**. The King James Version says she **dwelt** under the palm tree. This means she remained; she stayed; she abided. Deborah was still.

And yet, people still came to her to have their disputes decided upon, and their wrongdoings judged fairly. People counted on her, yet she remained still. Her stillness supported her people. In her stillness she was a steady pillar of consistency, reliability, and trustworthiness. *At that time* many others were scurrying and worrying, but Deborah was still.

KEY POINT: AS YOU ARE STILL, DISCERN THE NOISE AROUND YOU

We live noisy lives. And I am not talking about the humans in your house. I am familiar with friendly noise— come join us Harbins for a meal; we do noise well. To me that is good and bearable noise. The noise I am referring to comes from outside influences, threatening to penetrate the peace that passes all understanding. (Philippians 4:7)

A lot of noise can easily be avoided and controlled. We have the power and ability to turn off the television, shut down the cell phone, walk away from the computer, and cook more meals at home. For the moms in carpools who are running daily errands and taxiing the children, turn off the television in the SUV and make conversation with your kids. For those parenting teens create technology-free-zones and, in the stillness and quiet, have meaningful conversation, promoting deeper family connection.

Yes, there is noise we cannot control or avoid. Like the Israelites perhaps oppression is in your life. Literally, a strong, mighty, violent, pressing and squeezing cruelty that lurks and looms, harassing and hassling. Depending on the depth of the oppression, go to a Deborah and seek wisdom and counsel. Your Deborah may be a friend, a pastor, or a professional therapist. But above all, be still before the Lord and know He fights for you.

KEY POINT: DO NOT SEEK POPULARITY, PLEASE GOD

We live in a culture that promotes thinking of self, first. And yet how different is today's mindset from *in those days, everyone did as they saw fit*? Yes, if on an airplane should the oxygen mask fall, fit yours first. But in your everyday life, consider how many of your actions, motives, thoughts center on making sure *you* get noticed and having *your* needs met.

In this pursuit to fight fair, advance, get ahead, and be noticed, we must not lose sight of God. The Israelites lived among other nations and sects of people. They were influenced, enticed, and affected by other philosophies, principles, and spiritual ideologies. Perhaps they wanted to be liked, noticed, and involved with the Canaanites. And what is so wrong with wanting to fit in and take on their traditions, methods, and customs?

They avoided and neglected God's ways, trading them, disregarding them, for the world around them. They saw what looked good; they tried what appeared to work for others; they began worshiping idols and other gods. Yet the God of their fathers, Jehovah—the Existing One—will not be a pawn in man's pursuit of acceptance, honor, or esteem.

Living right accepts God's ways, honors the Lord, and esteems Him. We cannot do both; we are not created to be committed in two directions. We must choose one— please God or pursue cultural trends. Deborah was more concerned with pleasing God than seeking popularity and adapting to culture.

Personalities show distinction and prove the creative nature of God. We are not all called to be Deborahs: we are called to be still and allow God to fight for us. Regardless of our personality profile, we are expected to use the same qualities Deborah exemplified.

1) Be confident in the personality God specifically designed for you.

2) Be a mouthpiece for God.

2) Be a leader encouraging others to live right and

be still.

4) Be a mainstay; reliable and trustworthy.

KEY POINT: TO FIGHT FAIR, KNOW YOUR POSITION OF AUTHORITY AND WHEN TO BE AUTHORITATIVE

Judges 4:6 says, "She sent for Barak...and said to him, 'The Lord, the God of Israel, commands you: Go, take with you...and lead the way...' " Deborah sent for Barak, insinuating she is his authority. Let us not make this a gender-focused point, because that is not the point. Too many highlight the person and disregard the position.

In matters of human resource, when difficult discussions surrounding competency occur, it is advised to refer to an individual's position rather than his or her name. For instance, if Mr. Smith, the high school principal, is ineffective, as the school board discusses the matter, they would refer to Mr. Smith's position. "We have concerns regarding the high school principal," is preferred over, "We have concerns regarding Mr. Smith." Of course, at some point his name will be mentioned, but it behooves us to consider position before person in sensitive conversations.

Frankly, I do not care that Deborah is a woman. It is more imperative that she is a godly person, choosing to stand firm *at that time* when so many others are living contrary to God's ways. Deborah, the female, didn't send for Barak, the man. As God's mouthpiece and leader, His judge and authority over His people, Deborah sent for Barak. He was another Israelite choosing to live right amid the confusion, chaos, and commotion born from God's disobedient nation.

The name Barak means a lightening flash or thunderbolt. This Israelite, called by God for this specific

13

task, had an opportunity to be a flashing sword for the Lord. The word of God came to Barak, but it was Barak's choice if he would listen and obey.

Deborah is the God-appointed authority, and Barak respects the authoritative appeal from God's mouthpiece. He received the demand as if God Himself was speaking. Notice the three verbs Deborah uses as she quotes God.

- Go
- Take
- Lead

In Judges 4:7, Barak is further instructed by God, through Deborah, "I will lure Sisera, the commander of Jabin's army, with his chariots and his troops to the Kishon River and give him into your hands." We are not told the number of days it took for Barak to get to Deborah, but I imagine he spent time with the Lord as he walked by faith pondering the directive to go, take, and lead.

Was he thinking, *That does not seem like a fair battle! I mean, Jabin has chariots. Iron chariots! Unfair! Besides, he has treated God's people with utter cruelty, under unimaginable oppression. But word of Deborah has spread; her reputation is solid and what other choice do I have? I have wanted to help my people. I have been insistent that something, anything, be done to get us out from under Jabin's dominion. I am not sure what God sees in me that He would call on me, but if Deborah agrees, I guess I will find out how this unfair fight pans out.*

It is not about what we see in ourselves; it is what God calls us to that matters. There was a fight worth fighting; God chose Barak to participate. And He gave specific orders: go, take, lead. But before Barak acted, he went to Deborah.

"If you go with me, I will go; but if you don't go with me, I won't go," Barak said to Deborah. (Judges 4:8) God is Barak's ultimate authority, but the *ifs* caught him off-guard.

Barak knew God is sovereign, holy, just, and perfect. Yet perhaps seeing what appeared to be unfair meant Barak had his eyes on the opposing army; then his faith was not completely attuned to God's authority.

When teaching and training in leadership, many use the two-word phrase: leaders lead. It seems unnecessary to verbalize, yet there are many leaders not leading well. Politicians leading out of popularity, top athletes making dangerous decisions, churches tolerating sin, parents apprehensive to discipline and correction, friends unwilling to confront. The list is long. Leaders must lead well. Christian leaders must be led by God.

Like Barak, the *ifs* have carried me to places I didn't expect. I enjoy a girl's night out or a girl's weekend away. Years ago, I would meet annually with a specific group of friends. Oh, could we laugh and have a great time together! We all claimed to be Christians, though we were at different places on our faith journeys.

I recall one time, as the five of us were gathered around a pool, the conversation turned uncomfortable and ungodly—all in the name of fun. As a follower of Jesus, His Name should have more influence than fun. I had an opportunity to take the lead and stop the dialogue or walk away, but I thought **IF** *I leave, what will they say about me?* **IF** *I speak up what will they think about me?* The *ifs* won. I lacked boldness and said nothing.

KEY POINT: WHEN THE *IFS* WIN, GOD'S AUTHORITY WANES

The first words from Deborah to Barak reminded him who was in charge. The Lord, the God of Israel, was his leader. When God said *go*, there were no *ifs* included. God did not add the *ifs*; Barak did. Twice. On his long journey to Deborah, Barak had opportunity to deepen his faith.

The *ifs* from Barak diminished the spark God ignited in this thunderbolt, and they had Barak where God never intended—in negotiation. "If you go with me, I'll go, but if you don't go with me, I won't go." Barak was supposed to be gathering 10,000 men and leading those troops into battle. But instead, what appeared to be unfair had his attention.

Hebrews 11 is known by some as the *Hall of Faith* chapter. Throughout the 40 verses, many are named who valiantly and courageously fought the good fight of faith. In verse 32, Barak is mentioned along with a few other judges. Deborah is not named; Barak is. Should we focus on her obvious absence?

No! Instead, let us be encouraged by what the writer of Hebrews 11:33-34 says of Barak. "...who through faith conquered kingdoms, administered justice, and gained what was promised...whose weakness was turned to strength; and who became powerful in battle and routed foreign enemies."

Whose weakness was turned to strength. I am not insinuating we defend and even rely on the *ifs* because after all, God rescued Barak, so it will turn out just fine for us. No. I am persuading us to tuck in tighter to Jesus and trust God's directives. Yes, we will have weak moments. Like Barak, the *ifs* will lead us to places we never intended—questioning God's motives or actions and negotiating with the Deity are signs His authority is waning in our lives. But when we falter or fail, we must trust what we know about God, get back to the feet of Jesus, and remain still.

Before we know *what* we are fighting for, we must know *who* is fighting for us. Scripture is clear, Nehemiah 4:20 says, "...our God will fight for us!" In Deuteronomy 3:22 Moses declares, "Do not be afraid of them; the Lord your God himself will fight for you." Being ready to fight for the things worth fighting for, we must stand firm to see the deliverance the Lord brings. (Exodus 14:13)

Consider what you know about God. Who is He? What are His characteristics?

Like Barak, we get caught off-guard; therefore, we should be assured of God's character. Recently, I spoke at a women's retreat. In the middle of one session, I stopped talking, passed out post-it notes, had the women write down what they knew about God; who He is, what He says about Himself. Then we displayed them around the room, assured who God is.

When we doubt, question, or negotiate with God, there will be consequences and missed blessing. Through Deborah, God's direction was clear. He commanded Barak, "Go and take and lead." It behooved Barak to trust what he knew about God, walk by faith, and respond, "Yes, Lord." When fighting for the things worth fighting for, we are to fully trust our Authority.

It was not only the *ifs* that tripped Barak on his faith journey. Right in the middle of Judges 4:8, bookended by the two *ifs*, is a *but*: a lightning bolt for God flickered.

KEY POINT: DOUBT DIMS FAITH

There are things in our life worth fighting for; therefore, do not allow doubt to hinder or halt the battle. It is unknown who to credit for saying, *God doesn't call the prepared; He prepares the called.* Others say *He doesn't call the qualified; He qualifies the called.*

Followers of Jesus who try to ready themselves to fight for the things worth fighting for will fail to muster what's required for battle. God is clear; He fights for us. At times, He will call us to be a part of His battle plan, but He never expects us to guess His strategy. We are to trust the Faithful One.

Barak was commissioned for this mission. He was appointed by Jehovah, the God of Israel. As He commanded him to go, take, and lead, God was not looking for Barak to have his act together or his spiritual resume filled with accolades and accomplishments.

And God is not waiting for you to prove your faithfulness before He will enlist you into His army—fighting to deliver, rescue, redeem, or fight on behalf of your family or friends. He is ready to use you for His purposes, if you only trust Him.

But. This word gets in the way. It trips us, deceives us, and makes us doubt what we know to be true. *But* I am not good enough. *But* I can't. *But* I am too old. *But* I am not the right choice. *But* I will mess up. *But* is He sure? *But* I would rather do it my way. *But* did He forget what happened the last time? *But, if you don't go with me, I won't go.*

Barak's *but* did not have God in a frenzy, wringing His holy hands in a panic. He has the whole world in His hands; God is not wondering what in the world He will do now that Barak is negotiating the terms. Our *ifs* and *buts* do not deter God; they discourage, dissuade, and have us doubting what we know.

KEY POINT: EVEN IF WE GET UNDONE, GOD'S WILL, WILL BE DONE

In Judges 4:9-10, we see that God's will was done as

18

Barak's honor was undone. Deborah said, "Very well, I will go with you. But because of the way you are going about this, the honor will not be yours, for the Lord will hand Sisera over…"

God's will, God's way had Sisera being handed over to Barak.

God's will, Barak's way had him negotiating and his honor undone.

To fight fair, we must take our eyes off ourselves and keep them on God's will and His way. When we exchange God's way for our way, manipulating His strategy, a domino-effect of consequences occurs.

Disruption and fallout happens when we would rather do things our way and negotiate with God. God never told Deborah to leave her post. Disputes in the area could escalate in her absence. Times were volatile and unstable. Deborah was a steady leader; people looked to her and counted on her advice, wisdom, and adjudication. But when Barak negotiated with God's prophetess, it altered His original battle plan.

Even though—God's will, will be done.

KEY POINT: TO FIGHT FAIR, RECON MUST BE ON

Blindly going into battle is a huge disadvantage. Reconnaissance scopes out terrain, understands the enemy, and searches useful information to gain advantage in the ensuing fight. Before a military conflict, leaders hope to execute a reconnaissance strategy.

Know your enemy.

We may think our enemy is flesh and blood. At the root of all things worth fighting for are beating hearts:

marriage, children, addiction, friendship, extended family, health, finances, reputation, careers. However, Ephesians 6:12 tells us, "For our struggle is not against flesh and blood, but against the rulers, against the authorities, against the powers of this dark world and against the spiritual forces of evil in the heavenly realms."

People are not the enemy. Reconnaissance reveals though people are involved; they are not the source. We all have the same enemy. Satan. The devil. He is the enemy.

Kevin and I have six children. We adopted our youngest two when they were in kindergarten and first grade. Today, they are in high school. Their first few years of life were traumatic as they were abandoned and neglected by their birth parents. Biological father was only in the picture for conception. Biological mother was in a fight against drug addiction. Parental rights were terminated.

Yes, it is a sad story. Yes, our two kids are affected. But we want them to know, though their flesh and blood treated them poorly and chose lifestyles that shattered a family, their biological parents are not their enemy. Instead of casting blame, we discuss responsibility. Instead of pointing fingers at them, we talk about the real enemy. God's Word is clear—they are NOT the enemy and we must teach our kids the truth, so they are ready to fight the things worth fighting for.

Understand Satan's strategy.

Judges 4:13 informs us the enemy prepared for battle as Sisera gathered his 900 iron chariots and all his men. Since our enemy is prepared for battle, it is imperative we are ready to fight right.

Sisera came prepared for battle. And Barak was

aware of his enemy's tactics and schemes. Nine hundred iron chariots are a fierce force. Psalm 20:7 says, "Some trust in chariots and some in horses..." King Jabin trusted in Sisera and his mighty army. Sisera trusted in his iron chariots and horses. The chariots were threatening. The horses were daunting beasts. The enemy and his strategy were intimidating.

Trust your leader.

Military leaders gather their information from reconnaissance and strategize their battle plan. Not all troops are informed on the strategy; however, they are commissioned to trust the decision of the higher-ranking officials. It is their responsibility to show up for battle, ready to fight.

Barak went to the battle prepared. Yes, he had his moment of weakness, but in the end, he became all in. Psalm 20:7 goes on to describe how reconnaissance prepares us for battle. "...but we trust in the name of the Lord our God."

KEY POINT: LIVING IN THE PRESENT, FIGHTS FAIR

In Judges 4:14 Deborah congruently ordered and inspired Barak. If he was struggling with his past doubt, her charge of, "Go!" moved him from the past, set him in the present, and readied him for the fight. She did not remind him where he faltered, and she did not ask if *this time* he was ready. Instead, she motivated God's man with one word.

Her motivation brought inspiration. "This is the day the Lord has given Sisera into your hands..." *This is the day*—not yesterday, not tomorrow; God is on the move right now, so join Him. Then Deborah asked a vital question, "Has not the Lord gone ahead of you?" The only battles worth fighting are those that belong to the Lord. Barak can be inspired to go, advance with his 10,000 men and fight, because God was already there; His plan was set in motion. So, he went and followed God's lead.

In Judges 4:15-16, we read the sequence of events that happen next:

- Barak advanced.

Notice the change in this man. He was submitted to God's authority; he led well and was ready to fight, trusting God with his every step:

- The Lord routed Sisera and all the chariots and the whole army.

In the King James Version, the word for routed is discomfited. Based on the elementary rules of pronunciation, it would appear the second *i* should be a long vowel sound. However, this word steps outside the rule, and is pronounced as if there is a double *t*. It means to confuse, frustrate, foil, and utterly defeat.

Who routed, discomfited Sisera and his whole army, including the horses attached to the chariots? God did. How?

Judges 5:20-21 has the answer. "From the heavens the stars fought, from their courses they fought against Sisera. The river swept them away..." The powers of heaven engaged in the fight, suggesting a great storm of wind, hail, and sleet burst upon the enemy. Barak, the thunderbolt, was a witness to this incredible display of purposeful mayhem. He trusted in the name of the Lord our God while

Sisera trusted in his horses and chariots that were useless in a mudslide:

- Sisera abandoned his chariot.
  Leaders lead; they do not flee.

- Barak pursued.
  Followers of Jesus remain in the fight until God releases them.

- Sisera's army was demolished.
  Judges 4:16 says, "All the troops of Sisera fell by the sword; not a man was left." A grisly scene for sure.

- Sisera fled the scene.

Yes, he abandoned his chariot, but even worse, he abandoned his men, and then he bolted. In many countries desertion is a crime, and the penalty is severe during times of war.

It may appear the battle had ended. But God did say Sisera would be handed over, so rest assured, it happened.

One Sunday evening when I was about twelve, a lady stood up in church to tell of a time when God was at work in her life. Some details from that night are sketchy, but I will never forget her testimony. She spoke about her husband and how for years he was not a kind man. She said he was difficult to live with, but early in her marriage she met Jesus, and He changed her life.

Her husband did not meet Jesus; she did. She shared how she knew God had charged her with fighting for her marriage. She knew it was a command. So, she brought two weapons to this worthy battle—prayer and example. For 25 years she prayed for her husband to know Jesus, and in her marriage, she lived out the characteristics of a follower of Jesus.

For 25 years she did not leave the scene; she did not abandon her post; she did not pull rank, she did not desert; she prayed, and she stayed. And 25 years later her husband met Jesus. God promised her it would happen, and she trusted the battle and the outcome to Him.

I do not remember her face or know her name, but I will always remember the testimony of her fight. She remained at the feet of Jesus; she was still before the Lord and she trusted Him to go before her and fight for what He deems right. Unfair was not mentioned in her testimony.

According to Exodus 14:13, if we stand firm, we will see the deliverance the Lord brings. She was ready before the Lord, and she remained safe and secure in that fight for her man's salvation.

KEY POINT: ONLY WITH GOD ARE WE TRULY SAFE AND SECURE

Anyone fighting on their own strength is no longer covered by God's security plan. Sisera was running scared. But he thought he found his safety net in Jael's tent. (Judges 4:17) I am astounded at Jael's courage and fearlessness. Her temporary home, her tent, was within walking distance from a battleground. And Sisera, the commander of the most competent army in the region, fled to her husband's tent. Apparently, Sisera knew their location and assumed he would be safe and secure.

He thought wrong. Sisera could potentially depend on Jael's husband, but Jael trusted in the name of the Lord our God. Bold and gutsy, Jael went out to meet Sisera. Who was most ready? The commander, decked out in warrior gear, a massive sword still clutched in his hand, or a woman tucked in tight and led by the Lord?

According to Judges 4:18, fearless Jael bolstered a

fear-filled commander. Sisera was only trying to escape the sudden and deadly storm, but he had no idea the torrent that was about to downpour inside that tent. He started barking out orders to her, "Give me something to drink, stand watch, and lie if anyone inquires of my whereabouts."

Jael appeared to be attentive. She gave him something to drink and covered him up. It was all a ruse. Though her people helped Sisera before the battle (Judges 4:11-12), she was now ready to be used for God's purposes. She was ready to fight fair and help save God's people. She slew Sisiera.

Again, her gender is not the primary focus; her obedience and readiness were honorable and should have our attention. After all, Deborah did say the honor would go to a woman. Judges 4:21 records that Jael used a hammer to attach Sisera's head to the ground with a tent peg. Though the description of this account is riveting to some and revolting to others, *that* he died is the objective. Barak pursued Sisera to the tent and, at Jael's invitation, entered the tent so she could prove the demise of the commander.

Fighting fair is not about a fair fight. It is about a righteous God who calls on those who are ready to be used by Him in the battles He deems worth fighting for.

PONDER

deeply, carefully, and thoughtfully consider

1. Describe a time when you thought *that's not fair*.

2. Ellen says a part of fighting fair is to know that our enemy is not the people who challenge or hurt us. Name the people in your life who you have thought were/are the enemy. And then next to their name, write what it is that makes you think they are the enemy.

PERSUADE

God's Word influences, encourages, and guides

1. Read Psalm 37:7. What three things are we commanded to do?

    a.

    b.

    c.

2. Who fights for us?

    Nehemiah 4:20

    Deuteronomy 3:22

    Exodus 14:13

PRACTICAL

applying Biblical Truth to present day

1. How do Judges 17:6 and Judges 21:25 apply to our current culture?

2. On a scale of 1 to 5, with 5 being high, rank how well you do overall with the qualities Ellen highlighted regarding Deborah.

   _____ confident in the personality God gave you

   _____ speaking truth

   _____ encouraging others to live right

   _____ reliable and trustworthy

3. How can Psalm 20 be used as reconnaissance to fight fair for the things worth fighting for?

PERSONAL
inviting Jesus into your current reality

1. In Judges 14:8 the *ifs* caught Barak off-guard. What *ifs* have done a sneak attack in your life?

2. What current, unfair reality needs you to be ready to fight? What needs to change for you to fight right?

2
be ready to fight when WEAK

"The Spirit helps us in our weakness..."
Romans 8:26a

*"Red rover, red rover, send _____ on over." Fill in the blank with the name of the biggest and strongest kid on the playground. Oh, how I hated this game. But there I was, average height and weight for a third grader. my light-blonde hair held back by a headband, feet firmly planted on the ground, and both arms linked with two other eight-year-olds. We were waiting for **him** to charge across the playing field, ram his body against our connected team, and attempt to break the human chain. Like a bull preparing to charge, I imagined him pawing the ground with his foot.*

*Why had we called **him** over so soon into the game anyway? What a dumb decision. We had all played with **him** before. And we all had hopes we would land on his team.*

Before he dashed forward, I knew exactly where he was headed—to the weakest link. Me! Seconds later, as I sat on the ground, slightly dazed, but not at all surprised that I *was no longer linked with my classmates, I proved the proverb true, **a chain is only as strong as its weakest link**.*

Hardships, challenges, crises, and brokenness require our readiness. Ready to face the hardships and challenges. Ready to fight right through the crises and brokenness. After all, ready or not, like the burly boy rushing toward my skinny arms, here they come.

Deborah, Barak, and Jael were victorious over King Jabin and Sisera. Their obedience to fight right and fair ushered in 40 years of peace. But Judges 6:1 begins, "Again, the Israelites did evil in the eyes of the Lord…" There was no need for their enemy to chant *send them on over.* "… and for seven years (God) gave them into the hands of the Midianites."

Here they go again.

Remember, this was during the time when everyone did as they saw fit. It was a slow fade, but they swapped peace for evil practices. And God handed them over to Midian, meaning strife. Dictionary.com defines strife as discord, antagonism, and bitter conflict. When God established covenant with the Israelites, He promised blessing and protection if they served Him, loved Him, observed His commands, and walked in all His ways.

But they faltered. They failed. They stopped following the Promise Keeper and forgot the Lord their God. And God was clear—disobey and break His commands, and there would be consequences. Deuteronomy 8:19 says, "If you ever forget the Lord your God and follow other gods and worship and bow down to them…you will surely be destroyed."

The Israelites experienced destruction in their land, within their tribes, and certainly in their relationship with God. They were weak and needed to be brought back and tucked in tight to the Lord. Now that was a fight worth fighting for.

KEY POINT: ULTIMATELY, GOD CALLS US TO FIGHT, BUT IT IS ALSO OKAY TO VOLUNTEER

When was the last time you volunteered to fight for something worth fighting for? Throughout the Bible people stood up and fought. Let us not see these fights as a schoolyard bicker, or a fist-flying brawl, or an old-west-style standoff, or a march at a capitol building. Those are fights rooted in opinion, bias, politics, and selfish ambition.

Marital issues, broken friendships, wayward children, emptiness, a shocking diagnosis, death, age, debilitating circumstances—the list goes on. Christians are weakened from anxiety, the past, unforgiveness, addiction, and bitterness. Again, a shortened list. Weakness affects people. Weakness surrounds us. I know and love people who are weak. And they are worth fighting for.

Years ago, a friend shared with me about her husband's addiction to pornography. She was so weak she could not verbalize her emotion. But I could. I volunteered to fight on her behalf. Together we fought for her marriage and for her man. It took time. It was exhausting, and at times, excruciating. But he eventually responded to the battle. God rescued and redeemed the man and their marriage.

There have been times when I was not a willing volunteer. Apprehensive, stubborn, even belligerent. Days, weeks, months have gone by, and though I do not utter the word, my *no* is a silent resounding gong. God is the one who appeals, assigns, and affirms the battles we are called to, so any *no* that follows His holy summons affects our relationship with our Father.

Unwillingness to heed a call from God to fight for the things He deems worth fighting for triggers weakness. We need to fight against the unwillingness. We need to have our eyes opened to the opportunities God has for us and volunteer to fight alongside another who is weak.

KEY POINT: WEAKNESSES ARE NOT TROPHIES TO DISPLAY; THEY ARE OPPORTUNITIES FOR THE STRENGTH OF JESUS TO BE ON DISPLAY

Christian writers and speakers talk often about their weaknesses. I pay attention to their various platforms. Sadly, a lot of the time, I am discouraged. Unlike Paul, their message is more about their weakness and less about the strong Name of Jesus. It is like they are honored to wear the weakness and obliged to have the cross to bear. When we adjust our lives to the highlighted weaknesses, we make space for them and welcome them like invited guests.

2 Corinthians 12:9-10 says, "My grace is sufficient for you, for my power is made perfect in weakness. Therefore, I will boast all the more gladly about my weaknesses, so that Christ's power may rest on me. That is why for Christ's sake, I delight in weaknesses..."

The original language of the New Testament is Greek. In 2 Corinthians 12:9, one word is used for made and perfect. *Teleioo* means to accomplish or carry something through to completion; it is to add what is missing in order to render it full. Paul is not referring to any act of sin. The things God clearly labels as sin, we cannot call a weakness. For instance, if someone were to identify and gladly tell others that gossip, or worry, or impatience is his or her weakness, they would be wrong.

Without Jesus, we are incomplete. Without Jesus, we are lost. Without Jesus, we are empty. Only in Him do we find and know hope, peace, and joy. We wear skin; therefore, we are flawed. By nature, we are weak. Any mental or emotional strength we try to muster on our own will not last.

Only His power can explode into us and make us strong. Paul originally wrote this passage of Scripture as a letter to Christians. He's testifying to how God worked in his own weakness. "…That is why for Christ's sake I delight in weaknesses…" (2 Corinthians 12:10)

If we are leaning into our weaknesses more than we are tucking in tight to Jesus, we change the main character of the phrase, and it becomes more like *that is why for my sake I delight in weaknesses*. The question for each of us is necessary; does my weakness point to me or to Jesus?

If we are going to apply this passage to our lives, we need to apply the rest of verse ten. You see, Paul desired and intended the power of Jesus be displayed *IN* weaknesses, *IN* insults, *IN* hardships, *IN* persecutions, *IN* difficulties. The next question is equally necessary. Are insults, hardships, persecutions, and difficulties also welcomed guests on my faith journey?

2 Corinthians 12:10 ends with a statement that contradicts yet expresses a possible truth. Paul's paradox says, "For when I am weak, then I am strong." When we give our weaknesses, insults, hardships, persecutions, and difficulties to the Lord, then His power can be ignited and His strength explodes, trading our inability for His capability.

In the beginning of Judges 6, we see human weakness on display. The Israelites allowed the surrounding cultures to influence their lifestyles: most notably, what, how and whom they will worship. They have exchanged a peaceful reality for an oppressive existence. We are not told who volunteered in the fight for this nation to turn back to

God, but there would have been a remnant of faithful followers who prayed God to keep them strong as they remained and fought for their nation to return to Him.

In Judges 6:7 the Israelites cried out to God because of the intense oppression by the Midianites. Be assured, God knows crying from whining. God turns His ear to honest cries. "The Lord is near to the brokenhearted and saves those who are crushed in spirit." (Psalm 34:18) Whiners are not broken and crushed; they are frenzied and foolish.

God responds to sincere cries. Judges 6:8-10 records what God said through His unnamed prophet.

He reminded them:

- The Lord is their Lord.
- He delivered them from bondage.
- He protected them from a powerful enemy.
- He provided a place for them to live.
- He instructed them with worship guidelines.

He rebuked them:

- You have not listened to me.

KEY POINT: GOD'S HELP IS CONNECTED TO GOD'S COMMANDS

The Israelites wanted His aid but not His direction. They wanted His protection but not His instruction. They wanted His rescue without His rules. The unnamed prophet did not give them what they expected, but rest assured, God heard their cries, and as a Promise Keeper He would fight for His people. But a just and loving Father knew what His children needed. In this case recall and rebuke.

The prophet reminded the Israelites what God had

done for them. Notice the verbs used in the bullet points mentioned. Delivered. Protected. Provided. Instructed. God's ambassador prompted these people to reminisce. Recalling divine deliverance, holy protection and provision, and godly instruction reminded God's people where they belonged. When God had their attention, rebuke followed the recall.

Reproof is a powerful method of help. God's help comes through correction and strong disapproval. He is a good Father; therefore, He corrects. He is a loving Father; therefore, He lets His children know when He disapproves of how they are living.

Over the course of time, God's people became weak. They leaned on their own understanding instead of tucking in tight to His commands. They swapped sacred protection for manmade shelter. (Judges 6:2) They traded the fear of the Lord for Midian's invasion and intimidation. (Judges 6:3-6)

But God heard and responded to their cries and sent this unnamed prophet to communicate His heart. God's help and His commands go hand in hand. He promised He would be their God *if* they served Him, loved Him, observed His commands, and walked in all His ways. Yet they failed. But He also promised He would return to His children *if* they returned to Him. (Zechariah 1:3)

So, God called on one man to lead this fight worth fighting for:

- The man: Gideon. (Judges 6:11-12)
- The fight: Save Israel. (Judges 6:14)

KEY POINT: BEING SURPRISED DOES NOT MEAN WE SHOULD NOT BE READY

Judges 6:11 informs us that an angel of the Lord came and sat down under an oak tree as Gideon was threshing wheat. Gideon was alone, and God showed up. In the middle of an ordinary day, God revealed Himself to Gideon. It does not appear he was surprised by God's messenger.

When the angel of the Lord appeared to Mary (Luke 1:30) he said, "Do not be afraid." Likewise, the night Jesus was born, an angel of the Lord began the message to the shepherds the same way (Luke 2:10). Mary and the shepherds were ready for the message, but they needed their fears calmed to listen to the messenger.

Judges 6:12 reveals the message for Gideon. "The Lord is with you, mighty warrior." As we read Gideon's reply, we see he was not afraid of the messenger; rather, he was not ready for the message. "But, sir, if…why…where…did not…but now…" (Judges 6:13)

Perspective matters. Being on the receiving end of Midian's mayhem was Gideon's vantage point. Prior to God sending the unnamed prophet, the Israelites cried out to the Lord *because of Midian*. Understanding comes through proper perspective. Gideon responds to the message through the lens of the mayhem. Gideon was not ready for God's message because the but, if, why, where, did not, and but now blocked his understanding.

Mayhem may not be controllable, but followers of Jesus do not need to be controlled by the mayhem. Chaos and confusion, bedlam and bad news can rain down on our lives, but they should never reign over our lives. Because the turmoil had his attention, Gideon was not ready for the message. He doubted the messenger and countered with retorts:

Gideon's retort: *If the Lord is with us…*

God's revelation: *So do not fear, for I am with you.* **(Isaiah 41:10)**

Gideon's retort: *...why has all this happened to us?*

God's revelation: *For I know the plans I have for You.* **(Jeremiah 29:11)**

Gideon's retort: *Where are all His wonders that our fathers told us about?*

God's revelation: *Look at the nations and watch and be utterly amazed. For I am going to do something in your days that you would not believe, even if you were told.* **(Habakkuk 1:5)**

Gideon's retort: *But now the Lord has abandoned us...*

God's revelation: *I will never leave you nor forsake you.* **(Joshua 1:5b)**

Gideon's retort: *...and put us in the hand of Midian*

God's revelation: *If your heart turns away and you are not obedient, and if you are drawn away to bow down to other gods and worship them, I declare to you this day that you will certainly be destroyed.* **(Deuteronomy 30:17-18)**

When God has our undivided attention, we will listen to His message and trust His call, ready to fight any battle God assigns.

KEY POINT: GOD CALLS YOU WHAT HE WANTS YOU TO BECOME

Gideon heard God when He called him *mighty warrior*. God did not call Gideon what He saw in Gideon; God commissioned Gideon for the call He had on his life. The Lord knew the ensuing fight that was necessary to defeat the Midianites, so He chose and appointed Gideon as His mighty warrior. And then He began to prepare Gideon to be what He called him: *a mighty warrior*.

Remember, God does not call the prepared; He prepares the called. Gideon was not prepared for mighty status or warrior rank. But he was not supposed to be. God calls us to be ready, and then, He prepares the readied.

In Judges 6:14, the man, Gideon, heard the call and the commission to participate in what God deemed was a worthy fight. "Go in the strength you have and save Israel out of Midian's hand."

Save Israel? Israel had been under Midian's oppression for seven years! That was a tall order, a seemingly impossible task. Other versions say rescue or deliver Israel. It means to save them from their moral troubles and be victorious. The Bible in Basic English says, "...be Israel's savior from Midian..." It was not that Gideon did not believe this needed to happen, because he did. His struggle was that he could not believe God thought he was the best choice. He knew his weaknesses, and there was no way this weak man could be a mighty warrior.

And he was right. He was weak, and he could not make himself become a mighty warrior.

So the retorts continued. Judges 6:15 says, "But Lord, how can I save Israel? My clan is the weakest...and I am the least in my family." There is a difference between stating facts and challenging or doubting or questioning

God's call. It is true his clan was weak. It is a fact, in his family, he was young and seen as insignificant. But how his clan ranked and what his family, his community, and his friends saw him as, or even how he viewed himself, was not contingent on God's call and commission.

Some think Gideon was more focused on creating a flight plan than being ready to hear God's fight plan. Would he rather flee than fight? Was he trying to change God's mind?

1 Samuel 15:29 says, "He who is the Glory of Israel does not lie or change his mind; for he is not a man that he should change his mind." Gideon was not trying to change God's mind; rather, God was changing Gideon. God was preparing Gideon. God was making Gideon a mighty warrior.

Yes, the man lobbed another retort at the Lord. But Gideon's pitch was not meant to strike the call. When he asked how he was not doubting; he was wondering. You see, Gideon had heard all the words the angel spoke. Before he was called *mighty warrior*, the angel began *The Lord is with you*. And in Judges 6:14, after Gideon tossed one retort after another, God said, "Go in the strength you have..."

What? Did He say, "In the strength *you have*"? Does He mean, "In the strength *I'll give*"? Since God cannot change His mind, He did not make a mistake. He says what He means, and He means what He says. Gideon already had the strength he needed, because Gideon was face-to-face with a mighty God. A super-sized call required God-sized strength. So the Lord prepared Gideon by being His strength.

Gideon did not have to wait for God to become his strength; He already *was* Gideon's strength. And because He is the same yesterday, today, and forever, (Hebrews 13:8) His Word says He remains the same. (Psalm 102:27)

God is also *our* strength. Whatever your weakness right now, God is your strength. Whatever task He has called you to, He is your strength. Perhaps we pray more diligently for God to remove our weaknesses instead of diligently trusting God to be what He says He is—our strength.

In 1827, Anna Bartlett Warner was born to a wealthy and prestigious family. When Anna was young, her mother died. During the Panic of 1837, when she was ten, her father lost his fortune and the family mansion and moved to a ramshackle farmhouse near West Point, New York. To earn money Anna and her sister began writing. Together they published over 100 books.

Shortly after the family's devasting loss, Anna met Jesus. As an adult God called and commissioned her to lead Bible studies for the cadets at West Point. The words to one of Anna's songs were often sung by soldiers on military duty.

Jesus loves me! This I know,
For the Bible tells me so;
Little ones to Him belong;
*They are **weak**, but He is **strong**.*
Yes, Jesus loves me!
Yes, Jesus loves me!
Yes, Jesus loves me!
The Bible tells me so.

Arguably, "Jesus Loves Me" is one of the most popular Sunday school songs of all time. Soldiers on battle fields and cadets preparing to fight for something worth fighting for were reminded, through a simple tune with deep insight, that when they are weak, He is strong.

It was not until Anna Bartlett's father lost everything

that she met Jesus and found all she needed. Anna and her sister are the only civilians buried with military honors in the West Point Cemetery because of their spiritual guidance and care over many mighty warriors.

KEY POINT: BE WILLING TO BE THE ONE

Anna Bartlett was willing to be used by God to do what He called and commissioned her to do. And long after her death, He continues to use her song to teach little ones the same message taught to many mighty warriors.

And Gideon, the least likely man from a weak clan, was also willing to be used by God. Weak but willing is still willing. Before Gideon asked how he could save Israel, God asked Gideon, "Am I not sending you?" And after Gideon stressed his weakness, the Lord assured, "I will be with you..."

God remained in a conversation with His willing warrior and continued to prepare and qualify and ready him for the impending fight. In Judges 6:17, Gideon asserts, "...give me a sign that it is really you talking to me..." The King James Version says, "...shew me a sign..."

It was seven years before Israel's sin landed them in the stronghold of Midian. That is a long time to not be in communication or communion with your God. Gideon needed assurance, a distinguishing mark and a miraculous sign that the angel truly was the Voice of Truth.

Like when the Lord said to Paul, "...for my power is made perfect in weakness..." (2 Corinthians 12:9) Gideon asked God to show Him that power. Because God is unchanging, His power remained consistent. The same power that hung the sun, moon, and stars in the sky is the same power that rose dead people to life. The same power that made a donkey speak (Numbers 22) is the same power that made a mute man talk (Luke 11:14) and a stuttering man preach. (Exodus 4:10-12)

The exact power that closed the mouths of lions opened closed wombs. It made chains fall, prison doors open, blind men see, sick girls well, and withered trees flourish. God's power brought down a giant with one smooth stone and raised up an eight-year-old to be a successful, godly king. This power restores, redeems, rescues, renews, revives, and resurrects.

When Gideon asked for a sign, he was not demanding God bring His show-and-tell item to class. He wanted proof it was God calling, and he desired to witness His mighty acts to persuade and ready him to fight and save Israel. God responded favorably, because He saw Gideon's heart and knew his motive was pure.

When was the last time you asked God to show up and show off for you? And why did you ask God to show you His power and to give you a sign it was His voice you heard calling or commissioning you to do His work?

Part of our preparation is being secure where we stand. To stand willing to fight, we must remain tucked in tight to the same promises God revealed to Gideon. *The Lord is with you* and *I will be with you*. Settled and secure between the promises of God allowed Gideon to hear, receive, and be willing to accept God's fight plan. "...and you will strike down all the Midianites together." (Judges 6:16)

KEY POINT: NO MATTER THE WEAKNESS, IT WILL NEVER BE GREATER THAN GOD'S STRENGTH

After he received a sign that it was God speaking, Gideon was challenged to overcome a burdensome weakness. Judges 6:27 discloses the difficult struggle, "...[Gideon] was afraid of his family and the men of his town..." God knew where Gideon was weak. He knew this weakness could cause Gideon to misstep on his faith journey.

Remember, God was preparing Gideon to save Israel, and the preparation plan was God's call. The same night God gave Gideon a sign He gave Gideon an assignment. "Tear down your father's altar to Baal and cut down the Asherah pole beside it." (Judges 6:25)

The fight began. Before Gideon was ready to rescue Israel, God called him to a worthy fight. Fighting for his family was a fight worth fighting for. Gideon did not feel ready, but because God does not call the readied, He readies the called. If Gideon remained stuck in his weakness, he would not have experienced or known the strength of God.

The mighty warrior had been called to a fight: take down and cut down. This was not a holy suggestion, rather a command from Holy God. Tear down, break down, break through, destroy, pull down—utterly ruin what is destroying your family. That is a fight worth fighting for!

The altar to Baal must go. Baal worship was common in the land. But it was never God's plan that any other god be worshiped in His land. God promised this land to Abraham. Years later, Abrahams grandson, Jacob, and his twelve sons, landed in Egypt. Hundreds of years after that God called Moses to deliver His people out of Egypt and take possession of the promised land. Moses led the people out of Egypt, but they wandered in the wilderness for many years, never entering the land. After Moses died God called Joshua to lead Israel into the Promised Land (referred to as Canaan).

The Canaanites worshiped Baal: their god, their lord. He was worshiped because they believed he gave fertility to the womb and rain to the soil. Baal statues were symbols of fertility and strength. Prostitution and child sacrifice were common in Baal worship.

That's not easy to read or comprehend. God's people became influenced by this culture, and it infiltrated their families. Judges 1:28 says, "When Israel became strong, they pressed the Canaanites into forced labor, but they never drove them out completely."

Said a different way: *as Israel was focused on their strength, their weakness surfaced.* Judges 2:19 describes the outcome of *they never drove them out completely.* "...the people returned to ways even more corrupt than those of their fathers, following other gods, serving and worshiping them. They refused to give up their evil practices and stubborn ways."

God commanded a weak and fear-filled man, who He called a mighty warrior, to the task of tearing down and utterly destroying the very thing that stood in the way of his family's relationship with God. Gideon had his orders. Did he obey?

It appears he did. Judges 6:27 begins, "So Gideon took ten of his servants and did as the Lord told him."

BUT!

Smack in the middle of this verse is the conjunction hinting at a contradiction. "*But* because he was afraid of his family and the men of the town, he did it at night rather than in the daytime." This can be taken two ways. First, the same night God gave the directive, Gideon acted. Second, Gideon waited 24 hours, and then did as he was commanded. His fear is our focus, not the timing.

It is no different in today's culture. Families live with upsetting and unpleasant consequences when people refuse to let go or give up destructive practices. Families today are adversely affected when people choose their obstinate ways over God's way of living.

One friend of mine (I will call her Friend) was weak and fear-filled because an altar of ungodliness was in her home affecting her family. Friend began to sense something was wrong. She knew what it was, but she was afraid to admit it. Time went on and the altar grew, the evil practices accrued, and her marriage suffered. The computer, the altar. Pornography, the evil. Friend was anguished, but angry.

Friend listened to God. She took on the mighty warrior stance; God readied her, and she fought a fight worth fighting for. She tore down, cut down, broke down, and utterly destroyed the altar with a hammer and dropped the demolished computer at the curb. I have a picture of Friend in my mind standing tall, swiping her hair off her forehead, inhaling and exhaling one large breath, hands on hip, eyes on Jesus, loudly exclaiming, "Not in my family!"

Only through God's strength are we able to step away from our fear and fight right. Friend was weak. Gideon was afraid. But they were ready to fight anyway. Do not wait for the fear to go away before you are ready to fight right for the things worth fighting for. Stand ready on God's strength—weakness and all—and tear down, cut down, and utterly destroy, and kick to the curb, what devastates your family!

KEY POINT: DO NOT RENOVATE, REPLACE

Gideon's assignment was two-fold. Destroy, then build. This was not a renovation project. Gideon was not to restore or repair Baal's altar. He was to demolish it, and then rebuild a new structure. God said, "Then build a proper kind of altar to the Lord your God...using the wood from the Asherah pole that you cut down, offer the second bull as a burnt offering." (Judges 6:26)

Gideon did as God commanded. "In the morning when the men of the town got up, there was Baals' altar, demolished, with the Asherah pole beside it cut down and the second bull sacrificed on the newly built altar!" (Judges 6:28)

A thorough investigation indicted Gideon, son of Joash. (Judges 6:29) And the men of the town demanded Gideon's death. (Judges 6:30) Fighting right may not be popular, but it is godly.

Old foundations are not always sturdy and capable of handling a new structure. There could be no lingering lumber from Baal's altar touching God's worship table. Our hearts are no different. When Jesus takes over and we are in Christ, 2 Corinthians 5:17 claims, "The old is gone, the new has come!" Are you grateful God is not in the renovation business? Oh, He flips hearts alright, but His flipping is a complete rebuild—foundation and all.

When we are in Christ, God's character replaces our old traits. Our old identity is gone as Jesus becomes our identifier. Our old name is gone, and a new name is written down in glory. (Isaiah 56:5; Revelation 2:17) Old habits are replaced with new behaviors. Old passions are replaced by godly desires. It is not only our call and our commission to fight right; it is our duty and our responsibility.

KEY POINT: ALTARS ALTER LIVES

A mighty warrior can face the fallout without falling off his or her firm foundation. To stand ready we need to be on our knees. Fighting right for the things worth fighting for requires abiding at an altar of the Lord.

I often mention the altar from the church where I grew up. I have vivid memories of people walking to the wooden rails, kneeling in contrition to pray, seek, repent, wonder, ponder, change, or hope. They knelt for healing, wholeness, salvation, restoration, forgiveness, unloading, or revelation. The reasons are many. However, the purpose is worship with the outcome—altered living.

I saw marriages mended, attitudes and behaviors changed, families restored, and lives renewed. I heard testimonies of people who fought the good fight and watched people come to Jesus who some had said there was no hope. All it takes is one mighty warrior willing to build an altar and abide there.

One of my mentors, Beth, speaks of her green chair. It is her altar. Another friend, Jeanne, repurposed a spare bedroom. The whole space is her altar. My friend, Erin, has a small desk where she meets with God. The material and size of your altar are not important; hanging out and hanging on is beyond measure.

Others take note and get affected when we build altars and abide there. When the town demanded Gideon be sentenced to death, his father did not defend his son. Instead, he took a stand against Baal. "Are you going to plead Baal's cause? Are you trying to save him? Whoever fights for him shall be put to death by morning! If Baal really is a god, he can defend himself when someone breaks down his altar." (Judges 6:31)

For years, Gideon watched his father's relationship with Holy God weaken. Perhaps, it was a slow fade, and yet, still a fail. Joash was intrigued by culture, inspired by evil, and influenced by standards that were contrary to God's ways. Eventually, an altar to Baal and an Asherah pole replaced God's primary place on their land, at their homes, and ultimately, in their lives.

Someone needed to stand ready and fight! So God called His mighty warrior and readied him for that mission. But remember, Gideon's call and commission were to save

Israel. Since he fought for his family, he was ready for God to further prepare him to fight for Israel.

KEY POINT: PERSONAL POWER WEAKENS, BUT GOD'S SPIRIT EMPOWERS

Humans can muster fortitude, courage, determination, and strength. Individuals can marshal grit, tenacity, boldness, and stamina. But only the Spirit of God can empower His people to be mighty warriors carrying out His call and commission.

Personal strength was not meant to be enough, could not be counted on, and was never intended to be effective or efficient to save Israel. This God-ordained assignment needed God-sized power. Gideon needed more than human strength, emotional fortitude, mental stamina, or self-made power to fight this immense battle.

God's fight plan included empowering Gideon. Judges 6:34 says, "Then the Spirit of the Lord came upon Gideon..." The mighty warrior was now robed and clothed with God's Spirit. The Spirit of the Lord hovered and covered the weakest link. Gideon was clothed and ready to save Israel. He had to trust, listen to, follow, depend on, and obey the Spirit of the Lord.

A powerful, leading warrior brought 32,000 fighting men with him to save Israel. (Judges 7:3) But a mighty warrior, empowered with the Spirit of the Lord, trusted the number of soldiers God endorsed. Judges 7:8 says, "So Gideon sent the rest of the Israelites to their tents but kept the 300..."

In our weakness to stand ready and fight right for the things worth fighting for, a mighty warrior needs empowerment, not manpower. As Jesus says, "My power is made perfect in weakness." And Paul replies, "Therefore, I will boast all the more gladly about my weaknesses, so that Christ's power may rest on me...For when I am weak, then I am strong." (2 Corinthians 12:9-10)

PONDER

deeply, carefully, and thoughtfully consider

1. In Judges 6:14 God says to Gideon, "Go in the strength you have..." If God said that to you today, how would you respond?

2. Gideon felt weak, God saw a warrior. *I am weak but He is strong!* God called it like He saw it. He was also prepared to equip Gideon to become what He called him to be. What could God call you that you would have a hard time believing, but you know God is ready to equip you to become?

   I feel _____ God sees _____

   Explain:

PERSUADE

God's Word influences, encourages, and guides

1. Read Judges 6:8-10.

    What did God remind them?

    a. _____
    b. _____
    c. _____
    d. _____
    e. _____

    What was His rebuke for them?

    Where are you not listening to God?

2. What do the following verses say about God or Jesus? How can they influence or encourage you regarding weakness?

    a. 1 Samuel 15:29

    b. Hebrews 13:8

    c. Psalm 102:27

PRACTICAL

applying Biblical Truth to present day

1. Read 2 Corinthians 12:8-10.

    What baffles you?

    What bolsters you?

2. Read the following verses and directly apply them to a current weakness you are facing. Name the struggle and how the verse encourages you.

    Isaiah 41:10 _____

    _____

    Jeremiah 29:12-13 _____

    _____

    Habakkuk 1:5_____

    _____

    Joshua 1:5 _____

    _____

    Deuteronomy 30:17-18 _____

    _____

PERSONAL

inviting Jesus into your current reality

1. What weakness needs you to be ready to fight?

2. Are you trying to fight on your own strength?

3. What can you do differently to fight right?

3
be ready to fight when
WAITING

"I wait for the Lord, my soul waits..."
Psalm 130:5a

I am currently waiting. As I write Kevin and I are waiting for the pending birth of our first grandchild. I am at our summer place, and Kevin is home working. As we wait we are 180 miles apart. And our son and daughter-in-law are two states and 455 miles away. Time and space will not affect the wait.

So Kevin and I wait.

Eric and Rebecca have been in a unique waiting phase with this pregnancy. A growth scan a few weeks ago revealed their daughter is below average in size. There was concern for her apparent petite dimensions but not her development. Every two weeks the scan was repeated, but more often, baby's heartrate was monitored.

Eric and Rebecca wait.

Yesterday was the final scan. The medical team decided to induce labor since Baby Girl Harbin measured below the tenth percentile on the growth chart. Early on Friday afternoon they were admitted to the hospital.

Today, Saturday, I wait.

Life is filled with occasions to wait. Some bring contentment—like waiting in line for our favorite ice cream at our summer place. Other waits catch us off guard. Ten years has passed, yet I can still feel the unease when I heard my doctor say three life-altering words. "You have cancer."

Waiting periods vary. It is exhilarating to wait in line for a favorite amusement park ride. Last year, I was sorrowful as I waited for my mom to take her last breath. Nine years ago we were ready and eager as we waited for the case worker to call letting us know the names of the children we would adopt.

Waiting cannot be avoided, but how we fight through them matters.

KEY POINT: BE READY TO BEAR THE WEIGHT AS YOU WEAR THE BURDEN

In 1 Samuel chapter 1, Hannah learned how to wait. But it was not easy, and the wait lasted a long time because she carried heavy secrets in her heart. Hannah was bogged down by the weight of heavy burdens. If we are ready to learn from her wait, her story can encourage us to grow, challenge us to change, and influence us to live as Jesus intends.

In 1 Samuel 1:1-2 we are introduced to "...a certain man named Elkanah, who had two wives: one was called Hannah, the other Peninnah. Peninnah had children, but Hannah had none." 1 Samuel 1:3-5 gives further information. "Year after year this man went from his town to worship and sacrifice to the Lord Almighty...he would give portions of the meat to his wife Peninnah and to all her sons and daughters. But to Hannah he gave a double portion because he loved her..."

Two heavy burdens weighed Hannah down. She shared a husband and she was barren. First, in that day it was culturally acceptable for a man to have more than one wife. Though Elkanah was a godly man, he allowed culture to determine his stance, his actions, and his choices. Godly living is not based on cultural standards. To stand ready we must choose to be influenced by Christ rather than culture.

Second, Elkanah loved Hannah, but when she could not bear a child, he chose to take another wife. A covenantal God designed marriage. God's will must be done God's way. It was never God's intention for one man to marry more than one woman. Covenant is lived out between two, no more. Anytime we step off God's straight path of righteousness, we will stumble and face fallout.

Hannah's heavy burdens were glaringly conspicuous. What about you? Is the weight of your burden obvious? Or are they hidden well, buried deep, secretly weighing you down? We must be ready to bear the weight as we wear the burden.

KEY POINT: LIVING CONTRARY TO GOD'S WAYS, WEIGHS HEAVY

1 Samuel 1:6b-7 says, "...(Hannah's) rival (Peninnah) kept *provoking* her in order to *irritate* her. This went on year after year. Whenever Hannah went up to the house of the Lord, her rival provoked her till she wept and would not eat." (emphasis mine)

The weight pressurizes emotions

The Hebrew word for provoke means to be angry, vexed, wroth, grieved; to provoke to anger and wrath.Though not commonly used, vexed and wroth are onomatopoeias, words that sound like their meaning. Vex is to irritate and annoy. Wroth is stormy, violent, and turbulent. The King James Version uses fret for irritate. The Hebrew meaning is to thunder or rage. Bellows can internally and externally erupt and a brouhaha brews when one is caught in another's provocation.

The weight piles on

According to 1 Samuel 1:7 *this went on year after year.* For years, Hannah bore a heavy weight. For years, she was wroth from the wrath of her husband's other wife. Hannah trembled with rage, wept tears of humiliation, and wailed from grief.

The weight troubles relationships

Relations within the family were strained, but imagine what others thought of the Elkanah family. How many friendships were halted or hindered from the turbulence in this family? What did other families think as the Elkanah's strolled into town? If the weight of Hannah's burden was enough to cause her not to eat, then the severity certainly had a negative influence on her friendships. Worse, it absolutely affected her marriage.

The weight is woeful

1 Samuel 1:8 says, "Elkanah her husband would say to

her, 'Hannah, why are you weeping? Why don't you eat? Why are you downhearted? Don't I mean more to you than ten sons?"

Elkanha's questions were not to irritate her or annoy Hannah. We are told he loved her. 1 Samuel 1:5 says, "...to Hannah he gave a double portion because he loved her..." He did not ask out of ignorance or disregard. In fact he had high regard for his wife.

We must be careful and cautious as we read this verse. Careful to read it in context and cautious that feelings are not the filter. Feelings that will have the ladies gathering around a table on a girl's night out, gossiping about this man who appears to not take his wife's emotional storm into consideration:

How could he be so dumb? Really? He asks why she's weeping? Why doesn't she eat? Why is she downhearted, heavily burdened? Seriously? The man asks a weeping woman, weighed down by the long wait of suffering, why his love doesn't mean more to her than ten sons? Wake up, Dude! Hannah deeply desires a child; she's broken over this unmet expectation. She's a mess because his baby mama is making her life miserable. And he thinks a Double Quarter-pounder will make it better? Whatever!

See, before we can fight right, we must fully know if it is a worthy fight. I have been present when irritated and provoked women begin to share *what he did*. I have witnessed wrath-filled women, speaking on behalf of their wronged friend on *what he did* to cause her despair. And their defense is based only on what they have heard. Those ready to fight right search for more facts, look for missing pieces, and step away from their feelings.

The end of 1 Samuel 1:6 began this key point. To fight right, we must have all the information. If we ignored the first part of verse six, we would remain focused on what appears to be a husband lacking compassion for his hurting wife. We would be ignorant to the weight of their woes and not fully understanding the weight of Hannah's burdens. Imparting a piece of our mind when we only have portions of a situation does not stand ready to fight, let alone, to fight right.

For years, Elkanah was grieved as he witnessed the wroth and wrath from one wife to another. He married Peninnah for the sake of inheritance and legacy, but Elkanah married Hannah out of a deep, abiding, and lasting love. Therefore, her woes were his weight.

KEY POINT: UNMET EXPECTATIONS ARE AN ENORMOUS WEIGHT

The end of 1 Samuel 1:5 and the beginning of 1 Samuel 1:6 are difficult to accept.

And the Lord had closed her womb.
And because the Lord has closed her womb...

Literally, it means God shut it up. They are the same words used when God **closed** the place in Adam's flesh after He took a rib to create Eve. And it is the same Hebrew word used in Genesis 7:16, "Then the Lord **shut** them in" after Noah, his wife, their three sons and their wives, along with all the animals, were on board the ark.

God shuts doors. God closes things. We are intrigued to learn and read that He closed the open flesh in Adam's side. And it is a nifty trivia fact to know God shut the door to the ark. But we are uncomfortable and almost want to avoid hearing that it was God who closed Hannah's womb.

Our tendency is to focus on the closed womb more

than the closer. When we are burdened with unmet expectations, the weight of a heaviness hangs over our hearts. Being ready to fight right through unmet expectations requires we completely trust and solely rely on the One who closes and shuts things up.

God is sovereign and omniscient. Therefore, we should be longsuffering through arduous situations. Easy to say, challenging to do, yet, an absolute necessity on our faith journey.

We are not designed to withstand the weight of unmet expectations or heavy burdens. In these two passages from God's Word He teaches us how to wait, but intriguingly, no weight is cited.

Psalm 130:5 says, "I wait for the Lord, my soul waits."

Psalm 37:7 says, "Be still before the Lord and wait."

Both verses say that we are to wait and how we are to wait. We get so fixated on the weight of the burdens that we neglect to do as He says. Whatever the weight we are to wait for the Lord and wait before the Lord.

In 1952 the Reverend John M. Moore wrote the hymn, "Burdens are Lifted at Calvary." The refrain beautifully concludes, *Jesus is very near*. It is no secret Jesus hung on the cross, and He carried the weight of our sin all the way up that hill called Mount Calvary. And He takes away the burden of guilt and the heaviness called shame. Jesus and His cross bridge the gap between the weight of our heavy burdens and when we finally declare, "I wait for the Lord!"

KEY POINT: WAITING IS *STILL* WORK

Using still as an adjective, makes the key point clear. Waiting is not passive. Being still is active. Psalm 37:7

teaches how we wait, "Be still..."

During the months Jesus was in ministry many people sat still as He taught. There was a time when a woman named Mary sat still before the Lord. Luke 10:39 says, "Mary, who sat at the Lord's feet listened to what He said..." Being still offers perspective. Being still has no distractions. As we are still before the Lord, we are positioned to hear His voice.

Psalm 29 describes the voice of the Lord as powerful, majestic, and thunderous. It breaks cedars, strikes with flashes of lightning, shakes the desert, twists oaks, and strips forests bare. But after the trees fall, the storms cease, and all is calm, we can still hear God in His still small voice.

In 1 Kings 19:11-13, the prophet Elijah could not hear God in a great and powerful wind, or in an earthquake, or in the fire. After every noise settled Scripture says Elijah heard the Lord in a gentle whisper.

After Jesus died His followers waited. Between His death and resurrection, all was still. But God was still at work. The title and writer are unclear, but another old song proclaims *rolled away, rolled away, rolled away; every burden of my heart rolled away.* Like the disciples, we must wait through the silence. Followers of Jesus are commanded to be patient as we wait for the Lord.

It took intentionality and hard work for the disciples to be still after Jesus died and before the empty tomb was revealed. But just as the stone was rolled away revealing the empty tomb, if we are still before the Lord and patiently waiting for Jesus to show up in our circumstances, we will be ready to fight right.

KEY POINT: HEAVY WAITS NEED TO BE WORKED OUT

We all have challenges, hardships, and difficulties in our lives. The weight of the wait is heavy and burdensome. Some things require we wait until they get worked out and some may never be worked out. A loved one's death is final. Certain medical diagnoses or physical incapacities may not get worked out how we would like. Someone in recovery, or healing from a tragic accident, or someone fighting cancer may take weeks, months, even years to finally be worked out.

Like Hannah, you may be waiting for what appears to be a closed opportunity and you are praying and hoping for breakthrough. If we are still before the Lord, we can wait patiently for the heavy weights to get worked out.

Psalm 37:7 is a command, not a suggestion. Being still is not an option; it is a way of life. When we read God's Word as optional, we tend to do God's will our way. Elkanah was not still before the Lord; therefore, he was not working out his faith.

As a man of God, Elkanah worshiped God and diligently brought his sacrifices to Shiloh. His love for God is not in question, but his stillness factor is. He attempted to work out a self-made strategy rather than doing God's will God's way. As a husband he was burdened that Hannah could not conceive a child. As a man he wanted a son. He worked out his needs before working out his faith.

For followers of Jesus God provides a work-out plan. Philippians 2:12 says, "…continue to work out your salvation…" This verse begins, "Therefore, my dear friends, as you have always obeyed…" It is often stated, whenever there is a *therefore*, find out what it is *there for*. According to grammar rules, the word therefore is a conjunctive adverb. In this context, it demonstrates cause and effect.

The cause: complete obedience to God.

The effect: a working out of salvation.

Understanding the Greek definitions helps. To obey has two meaning:

1. To listen, to harken. It is like a butler who is ready for the knock at the door. It is his duty to listen and respond.

2. To harken to a command. It is to be obedient and submit.

To work out means *to do that from which something results.*

Jesus saves people. When we accept this gift of salvation, we are saved from the penalty and power of sin. Though sin no longer reigns, it still remains. Therefore, we must be still and listen for God.

When we work out our own plan instead of carrying our heavy weights to God and waiting before the Lord, we are not working out our salvation how God instructs and informs. We cannot work our way into a relationship with Jesus, but with diligence, we can work out our salvation. The Greek word for work out is a present tense verb. We are to work out our salvation not only when we want to and not only when we have time or out of convenience; rather, it is a continuous and careful and complete work out. And yet, our work out is absolutely dependent upon God working in us. Philippians 2:13 continues, "...for it is God who works in you to will and to act according to his good pleasure."

John Fletcher, a preacher and theologian from the 1700s said, "Good works alone evidences salvation." Good works on their own are not good enough to save anyone.

But once you become a follower of Jesus, any good work evidences what God first accomplished—the saving of your soul. And as you continue to work out your salvation, be still and unload on the Lord what weighs you down and keeps you from waiting before Him in full and complete surrender.

KEY POINT: WAIT GAIN IS WORTH MORE THAN WEIGHT LOSS

This key point is not about watching your weight. Waiting is a spiritual matter. Only as we wait before the Lord can we fight right for the things worth fighting for. In John 6:63, Jesus says, "The Spirit gives life; the flesh counts for nothing..." In His own words Jesus discounts our flesh as useless, disadvantageous, and worthless. Conversely, it is about what we spiritually gain when we wait well.

Worthy Wait Gain #1
Declare the Wait

Psalm 130:5 proclaims, "I wait for the Lord, my soul waits." There is no mention of the weight of any burden, only a wait gain. Like Hannah, we get weighed down by heavy burdens, and we ultimately need to make the same choice as the Psalmist—declare your choice to wait before the Lord.

As we wait, we gain.

Worthy Wait Gain #2
Take a Stand

1 Samuel 1:9 says, "Once when they had finished eating and drinking...Hannah stood up." As Hannah took her

stand before the Lord, the weight of her burden fell. Like Hannah, we can only wait well, when our burden is lifted.

Psalm 81:6 promises, "I removed the burdens from their shoulders; their hands were set free from the basket." Since burdens are lifted at Calvary, bring them to Jesus. After all, He is very near and He will lift the weight, freeing your soul to wait.

Taking a spiritual stand grows a godly backbone—a symbol of strength in character. Hannah did not take a stand against Peninnah or her unmet expectation. Instead, she stood up, ready to wait before the Lord.

Worthy Wait Gain #3
Weep, Not Whine

After she took her stand, Hannah wept. 1 Samuel 1:10 says, "In bitterness of soul, Hannah wept much..." Hannah did not bemoan, she bewailed. She expressed sorrow, not distress.

When we whine we are reacting to the weight of a burden. Waiting before the Lord does not require dry eyes. If your tears flow to Jesus, weeping is not weak. One who weeps, waits well.

Worthy Wait Gain #4
Pray

Hannah's tears flowed from her eyes as prayer poured from her soul. 1 Samuel 1:10 continues, "...and prayed to the Lord." In Matthew Henry's commentary written in the early 1700s, he says *Hannah mingled her tears with her prayers.*

Worthy Wait Gain #5
Keep Praying

1 Samuel 1:12 says, "As she kept on praying to the Lord..." Hannah's prayers multiplied and her faith grew. Hannah's prayers were widespread and powerful. Deep petitions and hovering and covering supplications are referred to as *prevailing* prayers.

Hannah also suffered through her prayers. In bitterness of soul she anguished and labored—unceasingly praying until new life was birthed into a circumstance. These are called *travailing* prayers.

Too often believers wait before the Lord and pray like we are in line at a fast-food restaurant. We place our order with the Lord, pull up to His holy window, and expect Him to hand over the requested item.

1 Thessalonians 5:17 commands, "Pray continually." That means incessantly and without ceasing. Intercession has no intermission. As you wait keep on praying prevailing and travailing prayers.

Worthy Wait Gain #6
Be Honest

Waiting involves honesty. We must be honest with ourselves and others. Hannah's honesty alleviated the weight and abetted her wait. In 1 Samuel 1:15-16, Hannah admits, "I am a woman who is deeply troubled." Though it is difficult, there is a sense of freedom when you open your burdened soul with a trusted confidant.

Omniscience cannot be informed, so be indubitably honest with God. Waiting honestly before the Lord frees us from the weight frustrating our hearts and minds.

Worthy Wait Gain #7
A Pour Soul Waits

Psalm 62:8 says, "Trust in Him at all times, O people; pour out your hearts to Him, for God is our refuge." Pouring out our hearts is to spill and shed. It is not a trickle or a be-careful-you-don't-make-a-mess as you pour. No! The Psalmist urges us to empty our hearts, to shed our troubles like blood gushing from a deep wound. According to this verse there is order.

Waiting well first trusts God. Once we are securely tucked in tight waiting before the One we trust, then we can pour out our souls to Him. After our hearts are emptied, our soul is sheltered.

Be careful you do not mistake a poured-out heart as a poor soul. Perhaps you have whispered, *Oh, you poor thing* or you have heard the murmur on your behalf. Eli, the priest, misread Hannah as a poor, inebriated soul. (I Samuel 1:13) Misinterpretation is not misrepresentation. Hannah was honest and prayed; she took a stand and she did not whine. She truthfully represented herself. At the end of 1 Samuel 1:15, Hannah confesses, "I was pouring out my soul to the Lord."

Waiting before the Lord is a poured-out soul, not a poor soul.

Worthy Wait Gain #8
A Lifted Burden is Weightless, not Absent

A burden left at the foot of the cross or laid at the feet of Jesus can no longer weigh you down and hold you back from waiting well. Hannah was ready to fight right and continued to fight through a long wait. She was freed from the weight of her burden, and a hole in her heart was filled.

Though her circumstance had not changed, she was still barren, but she was still before the Lord and waiting on Him.

KEY POINT: VOWS MADE TO GOD ARE SOLEMN AND SINCERE

I struggle when I hear people flippantly say, "I swear to God." Never mind what I feel; consider what Almighty God thinks about frivolous avowals. Waiting before the Lord, tucked in tight at the feet of Jesus, allows for solemn and sincere vows.

Hannah was deeply troubled, but because she emptied her heart onto the Lord, space in her soul was accessible and available for a transaction with God. The King James Version of 1 Samuel 1:11 begins, "And she vowed a vow and said..."

Hannah was not motivated by what she did not have. In sincerity of soul she made a vow. She did not swear to God so that she would get what she desperately wanted. No! This oath is all about what she would do should the Lord in His sovereignty assign her what she asked. To Hannah her vow was solemn and sincere. There was no flippancy or frivolity in her words.

She vowed a vow saying, "O Lord Almighty, if you will only look upon your servant's misery and remember me, and not forget your servant but give her a son, then I will give him to the Lord for all the days of his life..."

In Numbers 30:10-15 the conditions for a married woman making a vow are listed:

- If her husband hears about her vow but says nothing to her and does not forbid her, then her vow stands.

- If her husband nullifies her vow, then none of them stand.

- If her husband says nothing, then her vow is confirmed.

- If he nullifies them some time after hearing them, then he is responsible for her guilt.

Elkanah said nothing; therefore, her vow stood.

Our words and our word matters. If we say it then we should mean it. If we make a promise, we should keep it. Especially to God. Vows are serious, but culturally we amend, subtract, ignore, avoid, look down on, walk away from, eye-roll, and snarl at vows, oaths, contracts, and promises. Perhaps we do not consider the cost up front. For man-made, godless vows we may reconcile not counting the cost. But a vow made to God is binding—it is to be made with complete sincerity and absolute solemnness. What else would we expect from a covenantal God?

It is quite costly to uphold, protect, and preserve vows made to the Lord. Outside influences have us anything but still as we wait for the vow to be fulfilled. But, as we wait, God gives directives. He says to wait patiently and eagerly and with hope before Him.

I have vowed vows to God. Two significant vows involve my husband and my children. Over the years I have waited regarding my marriage and my parenting. At times I have waited well and other times I have not.

On September 24, 1988, I took my stand at the altar and vowed a vow about Kevin. To be clear, I vowed a vow *to* God *about* Kevin. My words of promise were directed at Kevin, but my vow was made to God. For over thirty years I have kept my word to God, but there have been moments when I have disappointed, disrespected, and upset Kevin.

God is faithful, and He has never failed our marriage. It is our responsibility to be still and wait before the Lord as Kevin and I continue to live out the vows we made to God regarding marriage.

Six different times Kevin and I vowed the same vow—to nurture our children in Christ's holy Church—that by teaching and setting an example they may be guided to one day accept God's gift of salvation for themselves, proclaim their faith in Jesus, and live as He intends.

Certain rituals vary across denominational lines. Baptism being one. My parents made the choice to have me baptized as an infant. Kevin and I chose infant baptism for our four older children. And in July 2011 on the Sunday immediately following the adoption of our two youngest children, Jaylen, who was seven, and Sukanya, who was six, were baptized.

For Kevin and I baptism is a binding oath between us as parents and our Sovereign God on behalf of our children. We publicly declared and asked for God's hand and grace to be on each of our children. We recognized it is not what saved them. We understood each Harbin would one day need to personally decide to accept God's gift of salvation.

At each baptism Kevin and I vowed vows to God about our children. We invited and asked God to preveniently be at work in their lives. We publicly declared our intentions by vowing to tell our children about God, introducing them to Jesus, taking them to church, teaching them to read, love, and obey God's Word, and by modeling a life of worship.

Baptizing our children is not a guarantee they will choose a life of following Jesus. Kevin and I agree with a favorite preacher of ours who says there are dry folks in heaven and wet people in hell. We are not responsible for the spiritual choices our kids make, but we are held accountable to the vows *we* make *to* God *about* our children.

It breaks God's heart when we flippantly make vows or offer oaths in His name and refuse to keep our word. Waiting well keeps the vows we make before God.

Hannah vowed vows. She counted the cost before she voiced the oath. She was all-in as a vow-keeper, bound to her word. Her ask of God was attached to her vow. She asked that God look on her misery, bring her to mind, and not ignore or forget her deepest desire. And should God respond favorably, she vowed to give her son back to the Lord all the days of his life.

Scholars believe Elkanah was a Levite, which indicates a priestly connection. This unborn son would, by blood, be in service to God. But Hannah took it to a deeper level. She consecrated and dedicated her unborn child to a sacred, life-long commitment. Sacred vows are not based on merit. Hannah could not, nor can we on our own ability and aptitude, do what it takes to fulfill a vow. Only God can qualify and accomplish it in and through us.

KEY POINT: THE WAIT HAS NO EXPIRATION DATE

Waiting is beneficial, valuable, and necessary for our spiritual maturity. As we wait our relationship with God deepens, and we are made ready to fight right for the things worth fighting for.

In 1 Samuel 1:17, Eli sends her off in peace and with his priestly authority, though he's unaware of what it is, he acknowledges her vow and approves her request. Hope dawned and peace settled as Hannah took Eli's words to heart.1 Samuel 1:18 says, "...Then she went her way and ate something, and her face was no longer downcast."

As we wait we begin to hunger for more of God. Like

Hannah, our spiritual appetites are restored and renewed. And others notice, encouraging them to also drop the weight of their burden and to wait before the Lord.

Waiting before the Lord has a proper response. In 1 Samuel 1:19 we are told, "Early the next morning they arose and worshiped before the Lord..." Hannah is where she belongs—worshiping God alongside Elkanah.

The verse continues, "...and then went back to their home...Elkanah lay with Hannah his wife, and the Lord remembered her." What a beautiful theme! Hannah was on God's mind.

Waiting well is well worth the wait. As humans we put expiration dates on things out of our control. If God seems distant we lose faith. If we do not get what we want, we doubt His providence. If trouble knocks at our door, we make room for the unwanted guest, and we question the sovereignty of God. Our trust in the Lord should never expire.

Jesus is the same yesterday, today, and forever. (Hebrews 13:8) The peace that passes all understanding stands as strong and sure today as it did when the Prince of Peace was born. In 1 Peter 1:3 God promises, "...he has given us new birth into a living hope..." This hope is alive; it is present tense; it is a joyful and confident expectation of eternal salvation. Jesus is living hope! And because He lives, hope never expires.

1 Samuel 1:20 begins, "So in the course of time Hannah..." When I read this verse, I love to pause. I am bolstered and encouraged by Hannah's wait. Hannah's need was met. God loved Hannah, and she was on His mind. Truth is, the love and the providential care of God is enough for anyone.

1 Samuel 1:20 continues, "...Hannah conceived and gave birth to a son." Did God give Hannah what she

wanted? No! God gave Hannah what He wanted! Enduring and complete joy is not based on our desires being fulfilled, rather it's found every morning, as we wait at the feet of Jesus.

God promises He delivers joy in the morning. (Psalm 30:5) Waiting is not hopeless, empty, or a time for despair. As parents it is our honor to pray our kids through the wait. It is a way to fight right. As our kids are waiting and they call on us in their pain, we must be careful not to rescue or offer solution. Too many parents become stumbling blocks to their kids, and godly lessons go unlearned. Do not rush your loved one out of their waiting period. Only Almighty God controls the timeframe of a wait.

Waiting is prime opportunity to seek God and have Him ready us to fight for the things worth fighting for.

Saturday evening, 11:48 to be exact, Kevin and I receive a text from our son. As his wife labors, Eric writes, "This has been harder than I thought. The pain has only increased, but it feels like no end in sight. Prayers, please."

Kevin responds to the text. "The pain ends when the child comes. Pain gives way to joy immediately."

Though we knew our first grandchild was a girl, Eric and Rebecca had not revealed her name. Two hours and four minutes later, in the early hours of a Sunday in June, their wait was over as Moriah Joy entered the world.

Praise the Lord! Their wait was over; Joy indeed came that morning.

PONDER

deeply, carefully, and thoughtfully consider

1. To you is waiting physical or is it spiritual? Explain.

2. Worthy Weight Gain #7 is *A Pour Soul Waits.* Would you say you say your soul is poor or pour? Describe how you have or can have a poured-out soul.

PERSUADE

God's Word influences, encourages, and guides

1. Read Psalm 130. In each verse write if it was an influence, an encouragement, or a guide for you as you wait.

    vs. 1 _____

    vs. 2 _____

    vs. 3 _____

    vs. 4 _____

    vs. 5 _____

    vs. 6 _____

    vs. 7 _____

    vs. 8 _____

2. Hannah and Peninnah behaved badly when neither had what they wanted.

   Read the verses next to the weight and then write how you can apply them as you wait.

The weight pressurizes emotions.

Ephesians 4:26, 29, 32

The weight piles on.

Romans 12:12; James 1:12; Luke 21:19

The weight troubles relationships.

1 Peter 1:22; Colossians 3:12-14

The weight is woeful.

Romans 15:13; Isaiah 35:10

PRACTICAL
applying Biblical Truth to present day

1. 1 Samuel 1:5 & 6 says God closed Hannah's womb. Imagine a friend coming to you for advice regarding a deep burden from an unmet expectation. Based on Psalm 27:4-14, what would you say to them?

2. Read Philippians 2:12-14. Paul writes that we are to continue to work out our salvation.

    How are we to work it out? (vs.12)

    Why are we told to work it out? (vs. 13)

    What potentially hinders us? (vs. 14)

3. In 1 Samuel 1:11 Hannah makes a vow. The key point says *vows made to God are solemn and sincere.*

   Why are vows serious to God?

   Explain why motive matters when making a vow to God.

   Describe why waiting is crucial to vow-making.

PERSONAL

inviting Jesus into your current reality

1. Burdens are heavy. In Matthew 11:30 Jesus says, "My yoke is easy and my burden is light." Write out your new weight-loss plan regarding any heavy burden you currently bear or will bear.

4
be ready to fight for your HOUSEHOLD

"...But as for me and my household,
we will serve the Lord."
Joshua 24:15

Since 1988, I have lived in thirteen different houses (fourteen, if I count our summer place.) Two of the fourteen were without Kevin, whom I married later that same year. That means, on average, I have spent 2.21 years in each house, with the longest nine years and the shortest, four months.

As a self-proclaimed, semi-professional mover, I've learned some lessons:

- Moving often does not allow for stockpiling. (*Who wants to keep moving those boxes each time?*)

- Furniture purchased for one house may not fit as well in the next.
  (*Consequently, our bulky dining room set.*)
- Embracing change is beneficial.
  (*I choose to see moving as an adventure.*)
- Pack books in small boxes.
  (*It took one move to learn this lesson.*)
- Pack items from the kitchen in plastic bins.
  (*Handles help, plus it adds color to the boring cardboard boxes.*)
- Offering opinions to the *official* movers requires diplomacy and tact.
  (*I may have learned this the hard way.*)

Perhaps the greatest lesson Kevin and I have learned from moving is that a household is not tied to a house. A house is a structure, a dwelling place. A household is a collection of people residing on the property. To fight right for our households, we must be clear on the difference.

KEY POINT: A HOUSE IS NOT YOUR HOME

Prior to adopting, though Kevin and I subconsciously understood this key point, we never voiced it. We refer to December 18, 2010, as Gotcha Day. It is the day Jaylen and Sukanya left foster care forever and forever entered our home. Six months later our address changed. (For Kevin and I that was move #10.)

Transient describes the first few years of Jaylen and Sukanya's lives. Seventeen months separate their birthdates, yet two different states are named on their birth certificates, and they landed in foster care in a third state.

Without a proper or decent family foundation, move #10 for us was just another transfer for them.

We did not want Jaylen and Sukanya to misconstrue Daddy's job transfer as another transient experience, so we quickly embraced the key point. What once went without being said immediately became imperative in many conversations and parenting moments. Over the years we have explained it better, but for their comprehension we simply said, "A house is what we live in, but our home goes with us, wherever we go."

At that same time our daughter, Christine, was a junior in college at a university in another state; our son, Andrew had just entered the Marine Corps; Eric had graduated and was leaving for his freshman year of college, and Troy was entering his junior year in high school. Jaylen was headed to second grade and Sukanya first grade. Our reality was confusing to their transitory mindset. Obviously, since that move, our older four kids have often changed addresses. But no matter where they went, they were still a part of our household.

KEY POINT: C + LEAVE = CLEAVE

Until leave and cleave became a reality.

Within seventeen months, on December 30, 2016, July 8, 2017, August 12, 2017, and August 11, 2018, we celebrated the weddings of Andrew and Taylor, Eric and Rebecca, Troy and Kaitlin, and Christine and Brandon.

As you can see, the first three ceremonies occurred within seven months. After my third son got married, I wrote the following blog post.

One Letter Makes a Big Difference

Leave. Defined, this word means to go away from
or to depart permanently.
What happens when a C is added?
One letter makes a big difference.
Cleave. Defined, it means to cling and remain faithful.
I had a front-row seat as I witnessed each son leave.
And though my seat didn't change, my position did.
In a split second of time, a blink of an eye,
a quick intake of breath, my sons took their leave.
For the C to be, it was necessary.
One letter makes a big difference.
My husband performs many wedding ceremonies.
He's very good at it.
It's the rehearsals he leads that I appreciate.
I've learned much from Kevin.
My favorite part is when the father-of-the-bride
escorts his daughter down the aisle.
Bride-to-be is on the left, groom-to-be is on the right.
Father-of-the-bride stands between both.
Kevin stops and brings attention to this formation.
Our three sons desired Kevin be dad for their weddings—
asking other special men in their lives
to perform their ceremonies.
Three sons, three different officiants,
allowing Kevin to have a front-row seat alongside me.
But I was reminded of Kevin's words.
He makes sure everyone is aware of Dad's position—
standing between his daughter and the man
who is not yet her husband,

He'll say something like, "Dad, you're still in the picture.
But something significant will happen
as soon as you answer
the 'who-gives-this-woman-to-be-married' question.
You'll place her hand in his, step back,
and you'll be out of the picture."
At our son's weddings I was keenly aware of this transfer.
Three times a bride's dad stepped out of the way.
And when he did my son stepped in,
where her dad once stood.
They took their leave.
When Andrew, Eric, and Troy took their leave,
they stepped into their new position
and immediately added a C.
And now they Cleave—Andrew to Taylor,
Eric to Rebecca, and Troy to Kaitlin.
Prior to their weddings my sons did well at
honoring and respecting their momma.
Many times, I'd receive a greeting
before their girlfriend/fiancé.
It's just how they did it.
Until they took their leave and added a C.
One letter makes a big difference.
Like the father-of-the-bride,
the mother-of-the-groom must step back.
Because another woman has her son's attention.
One letter makes a big difference.
Witnessing my sons promise a young lady's dad that
they would love, honor, cherish, and keep his daughter

'til death do them part,
brought great joy to my heart.
These girls are in good hands.
I know.
Because my sons took their leave and added a C.

On the days our four older children were married, four new homes began; new households were created.

When Kevin performed the wedding of our friend's daughter, he said something profound. In his message he said, "Children do not make a family. God does. Ryan and Rachel, today, your family is complete. Should children come, they will be an addition to the family God has established today."

KEY POINT: HOUSEHOLD FOUNDATION MATTERS

What a house is built on makes a difference to its overall stability. Likewise, the foundation of a household is an enormous matter of significance. Jesus Christ is a sure foundation. Without Him we are sure to crumble and fall. Before His Son's birth God provided a firm foundation for His people. He communicated expectations of a relationship with Him to guide their lifestyle, ground their faith, and shape their character.

When we live by those same tenets, we are steady and established. When cracks occur upheaval moves in. Should separation from the foundation happen, a household will suffer. If conflict takes up residence, space is made for the unwelcomed roommates called disunity and discord.

How do we fight right when our household is unsteady?

KEY POINT: NAVIGATE TENSION, AVOID DISSENSION

In 1 Samuel 25:2-3, we are introduced to a man named Nabal, meaning fool. We are told he is a very wealthy man who owned massive property for his herds – thousands of goats and sheep. His character is described as, "...surly and mean in his dealings." Though Nabal is a Calebite, he chose not to live by their reputation of decent morality or with righteous integrity.

The King James Version uses the word *great* for wealthy. The Hebrew definition of great includes loud and intense. Add that to surly and mean and an understanding of this man's character begins to form. Surly is churlish, meaning cruel, obstinate, and difficult. As a businessman, a neighbor, a manager, and in his household, he was evil. Nabal was unpleasant, disagreeable, malignant, unkind, unpleasant, and unethical. Inflicting misery and pain, he was bad to the core, the worst kind of man.

The theory, *opposites attract*, could be applied to Nabal and his wife. 1 Samuel 25:3 introduces us to Abigail. "She was an intelligent and beautiful woman." Literally, she was prudent and insightful.

Many will question her good sense and judge her insight based on her choice of a husband. That is not right. It is not in Scripture; therefore, we do not know how this couple met and married. Perhaps it was an arranged marriage. Maybe it was a business arrangement. It is possible he changed after they married or intentionally presented himself to be a different man prior to their nuptials.

I know of similar households where one spouse is the neighbor you wish for, and the other is the one you pray will move away. As we read and look deeper into Nabal and Abigail's story, we must be careful to read it at face value and not insert our preconceived notions or apply it to our individual reality. Their story is just that; it's theirs. And God saw fit to tell it in His Word for our benefit. If your husband is a surly man or your wife a mean woman, it is my hope that Abigail's life will strengthen and encourage you to be ready to fight right for your household.

Though tension is expected in any household, dissension is not. Tension comes from differing opinions born out of distinctive personalities and persuasions. Contention, opposition, aggression, and hostility precede dissension. For a healthy household dissension is unacceptable.

Personality tests prove how differently Kevin and I are wired. We need to consistently make intentional decisions for our household. We choose to navigate tension while avoiding dissension.

Nabal chose poorly, while Abagail navigated wisely.

KEY POINT: TUNNEL VISION BLOCKS PERSPECTIVE

We need some backstory to help understand what is about to impact Abigail and Nabal's household. At the end of 1 Samuel 25:1 it says, "Then David moved..." Then "hints" we should know why David moved.

This is the same David who was anointed to be king over Israel and who killed the giant, Goliath. Over some years King Saul stopped following God and was overcome with jealousy of David and his success. David escaped Saul's palace and became a man on the run from a king recklessly determined to capture and kill God's anointed man.

In 1 Samuel 24, we can read a story that grabs the attention of middle school boys. And yet, it is in God's Word so we can all glean from it. Basically, King Saul had been pursuing the Philistines, and he returned to his palace to receive news of David's whereabouts. The king selected 3,000 choice men to be his search party. (This next part is where a 12-year-old mindset is helpful.) So the king went into a cave to *relieve* himself. Nope. He was not tired. He did not need a timeout. He needed privacy to do the business of relieving himself. He assumed he was alone, but David and his men were hiding from King Saul in the back of the same cave.

David had the opportunity to confront and the motive to kill the king. In fact, his men encouraged the sneak attack, citing that this was obviously the Lord's handiwork. As David crept over to King Saul, he cut off a corner of the king's robe, but God struck David's conscience. And David said to his men, "The Lord forbid that I should do such a thing to my master, the Lord's anointed, or lift my hand against him; for he is the anointed of the Lord." (1 Samuel 24:6)

To be clear, God anointed David as His choice for Israel's king, but when the people chose Saul first, God allowed it, and he was anointed as their king. Though King Saul had turned toward evil ways, David refused to take down the king without explicit direction from God. With the cut-off piece of kingly robe in his hand, David walked out of the cave behind Saul, bowed facedown to the king and confronted him regarding his innocence and the king's ludicrous obsession for vengeance.

Just because we have opportunity to take matters into our own hands, does not mean we are being led by the Spirit of God. Like David, we can be pushed to the back corner of a difficult situation, narrow-mindedly focused on *I need out* and remember that God rescues His children from the prison of tunnel vision. And it is God who strikes consciences. He grabs our attention and widens our perspective.

It was after God struck David's conscience and widened his tunnel vision that David moved to the outskirts of Nabal and Abigail's land. In 1 Samuel 25:4-9 David sends ten of his men with a respectful greeting to Nabal, asking for a courtesy of whatever food is left over, could he please spare it for David's hungry crew.

Nabal built and grew a successful business and had a large household that included employees on his massive property and servants in the house. David knew of Nabal's reputation, but he also knew of his wealth. So David sent word to Nabal informing him of a previous time when he and his soldiers dwelled with his shepherds. The messengers told Nabal there was no mistreatment or disrespect of his land, his people, or his herds when David and his men were present on his land.

David's kind greeting was, "Good health to your household!"

Nabal's surly come back was, "Good riddance!" (1 Samuel 25:10)

It is so easy to get caught up in what's happening on our home front that we fail to see what is happening around us. Clearly, Abigail's homelife was complicated and challenging. And yet, explanation is not excuse for a lack of faith in God. Yes, she had a jerk for a husband, and he made life difficult, but she was still responsible for her own behavior and attitude and her consideration of others.

KEY POINT: PRUDENCE PROTECTS YOUR HOUSEHOLD

An elementary school teacher shared a piece of wisdom. There is a difference between tattling and reporting. Tattling wants to get another in trouble, while reporting desires to keep them out of trouble. Kevin and I instituted this wise advice as a parenting strategy. We dislike tattling, but we expect reporting.

One of Nabal's servants reported to Abigail what had happened between her husband and David's men. This servant had the entire household on his mind. Protecting the household was his motivation to report. He was aware of Abigail's keen insight and good sense because he had witnessed her prudence in action.

It is not common or desirous to be called a prude. But because the definition means to be exceedingly modest or proper, hearing "You're exceedingly proper" would be a welcomed compliment. However, character must surpass compliment. As followers of Jesus we should live properly; therefore, we should pray for prudence. Abigail was prudent as she fought for her household.

Prudent is wise.

Proverbs 1:3 says that the proverbs were written "...for acquiring a disciplined and prudent life..." The King James Version says, "To receive the instruction of wisdom..."

The servant made a full report. [1 Samuel 25:14-17] He told Abigail how David sent messengers with a greeting to their master, and Nabal hurled insults. He went on to say how good David's men were to them when they stayed with the workers. He told her David's soldiers were a wall of protection around the shepherds and sheep. The servant used prudence when he concluded, "...see what you can do, because disaster is hanging over our master and his whole household..."

Prudent is sagacious.

Sagacious! This is a new word to me. And I love it! It

means having and showing acute mental discernment and keen practical sense and responding calmly and sensibly, keeping your head in the game. In 1 Samuel 25:18 it says, "Abigail lost no time." She was sagacious. She responded with action to the servant's bold plea. A wise and sagacious woman fights right for her household.

Prudent is sober.

Sober is controlled. Sober has the right mindset. Sober is clearheaded. It takes intentionality to be self-controlled. Abigail refused to be wrecked and overcome by the servant's report. She showed remarkable restraint. Abigail had one thing on her mind: fight for her household. She immediately went into preservation mode.

1 Samuel 25:18 says, "She took two hundred loaves of bread, two skins of wine, five dressed sheep, five seahs of roasted grain, a hundred cakes of raisins and two hundred cakes of pressed figs and loaded them on donkeys."

Whoa! Only a sober mind can plan to provide, with only a moment's notice, for hundreds of hungry soldiers while preserving an entire household. Abigail kept her wits about her. She did not have time to create a plan or meet with the servants. The plan unfolded as she went to work. After the items were packed and loaded, she sent her servants on ahead of herself.

Too many followers of Jesus live overwhelmed lives, stuck in the mire or buried under difficult circumstances. To fight right for our households, we must be sober-minded, otherwise, like a drunkard, we become mentally and emotionally inebriated, under the influence of whatever has our attention. When we are crushed by the enormity of a situation, we are unable to fight right. Only through the power of the Holy Spirit can we think clearly and act soberly.

Prudent is discreet.

1 Samuel 25:19 concludes, "But she did not tell her husband." Alert and observant, she opted for discretion over secrecy. She knew confronting Nabal would have dire consequences. Abigail was not keeping secrets from her husband; she was fighting for her household.

Women who use retail therapy, or gossip about *what he did*, or think *see if I ever tell him anything again* are spiteful and self-centered. Discreet people are prudent, vigilant to fight for their household instead of driven to vengeance. Abigail chose prudence over vengeance.

After David's men left Nabal, they reported every word the surly man said. [1 Samuel 25:12] I realize they are not a group of third grade boys. However, I envision the ten men talking at once, elbowing one another to get closer to David; passionately, but not intentionally, igniting his anger. It seems more like a tattling maneuver than a reporting opportunity.

David was not prudent. Instead, he was reactive, explosive, and vengeful. "David said to his men, 'Put on your swords!' So, they put on their swords, and David put on his. About four hundred men went up with David, while two hundred stayed with the supplies." (1 Samuel 25:13) David could use a lesson in prudence from Abigail.

1 Samuel 25:20-22 says, "As she came riding her donkey into a mountain ravine, there was David and his men descending toward her, and she met them. David had just said, 'It's been useless—all my watching over this fellow's property in the desert so that nothing of his was missing. He has paid me back evil for good. May God deal with David, be it ever so severely, if by morning I leave one

male of all who belong to him!" Can you see how Abigail's prudent fight for her household was indispensable?

David is driven by fury; Abigail by prudence. This beautiful woman riding a donkey came face-to-face with 401 angry, hungry, sword-wielding warriors. But they were powerless against her prudence. They stopped in their tracks when she quickly got off her donkey, fell at David's feet, and bowed down before him with her face to the ground.

In a culture of texting and emailing without discretion and impulsively pressing *send* to comment or post on social media has consequences. Discretion should never become obsolete; therefore, we must model it in our households. To fight right, Abigail relied on this indispensable quality. She was not secretive, she was discreet.

Prudent is mindful.

A prudent person remains in a worthy fight. In 1 Samuel 25 it says she could have gathered her servants and their packed donkeys, left the supplies with the 400 men, and walked back home, but she was still fighting for her household. And she was doing it right:

- Abigail was aware. *She was willing to take the blame.* (v. 24-25)

- Abigail was attentive. *She stated her case with facts not feeling.* (v. 25)

- Abigail appealed. *She negotiated for the sake of her household.* (v. 26-31)

God used her prudence to stop needless bloodshed

and uncalled-for-acts of vengeance on her household. But the Lord also used Abigail's appeal to remind David of the anointing power and purpose God had on his life. "When the Lord has done for my master every good thing he promised concerning him, and has appointed him leader over Israel, my master will not have on his conscience the staggering burden of needless bloodshed or having avenged himself..." (1 Samuel 25:30-31)

KEY POINT: BEING SELFLESS, SAVES A HOUSEHOLD

Nabal's cruelty was overt and his hardened heart obvious. Malicious and calloused people are excessively self-absorbed. If selfish were all the way to the left and selfless was to the far right, Nabal and Abigail would be at opposite ends of that spectrum. This is not an example of opposites attract or differences balancing each other. This is a case of wickedness wrecking a household and a woman refusing to accept the wreckage.

We must be ready to fight against wickedness in our households. It should never be defended or endorsed. If we claim exhaustion, defend the menace, or ignore wicked ways, we too are selfishly wrong. Two wrongs are not ready to fight right.

To combat selfishness, we must take a selfless stand. Before we are ready to fight, we must see if any selfish ways are present. Ask yourself:

- Do I demand or declare my rights?
- Do I throw pity parties for me, myself, and I?
- Do I pray primarily in first person?
- Do I pray monologue prayers?

Even though Abigail lived with a narcissistic fool, she was still responsible for her reactions and responses to Nabal's vicious ways. She chose the selfless road and was ready to do what was necessary to save her household.

KEY POINT: CONFRONT, DO NOT BE CONFRONTATIONAL

Selfless and prudent followers know the difference between confronting and being confrontational. Most people do not dwell in a hostile household, but every household needs a healthy understanding of confrontation. Confronting is not about being heard or making your point; it is for the benefit of the whole household. Abigail knew this.

1 Samuel 25:36 begins, "When Abigail went to Nabal..." She initiated the confrontation. The verse continues, "...he was in the house holding a banquet like that of a king. He was in high spirits and very drunk." Abigail did the right thing. A sense of satisfaction could have come through lambasting her fool husband in front of the partiers. Satisfaction without righteousness is empty; therefore, the confrontation would have turned confrontational in a heartbeat.

Regarding marital mayhem, I once heard the well-known speaker, writer, and Bible teacher Beth Moore say something like, "Stop fighting with your man, and start fighting for your marriage." Beth is right! Wives waste time fighting with their men. Ladies, what would happen in your household if you implemented a new fight plan with a useful confrontation strategy?

In most homes women are the barometer of the household. If we use *you* statements as we confront, then we are being confrontational. You are the worst! You are so wrong! You make me so mad! Highlighting anger fuels fury.

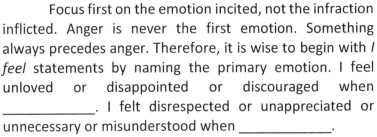

Focus first on the emotion incited, not the infraction inflicted. Anger is never the first emotion. Something always precedes anger. Therefore, it is wise to begin with *I feel* statements by naming the primary emotion. I feel unloved or disappointed or discouraged when _____. I felt disrespected or unappreciated or unnecessary or misunderstood when _____.

Abigail remained controlled and selfless. The end of 1 Samuel 25:36 says, "So she told him nothing until daybreak." As parents and friends, at your church or in the workplace, within organizations or communicating with neighbors, carefully calculated confrontations allow for purposeful conversation.

KEY POINT: WHEN GOD IS HANDS-ON, OUR HANDS ARE OFF

God is sovereign and providential. He has supreme authority, omnisciently and carefully guiding and directing His children. When we surrender to His ways, we are recipients of His sovereignty and divine providence. To fight right for our households, we must have our hands off what God has His hands on.

We pray for God to touch our family, intervene in our marriage, guide our parenting, and provide for our needs. And our prayers are sincere. Have you ever petitioned the Lord but quickly took control back? If God reigns over your household, your prayer should be *Holy Spirit, rein me in, and please reign in me*.

Abigail was reined in, tucked in tight, and trusting Almighty God. 1 Samuel 25:37 reports, "Then in the morning, when Nabal was sober, his wife told him all these things, and his heart failed him and he became like a stone." The foolish man had no idea how close to ruin he was as his prudent wife saved his life from David's sword. Commentator Matthew Henry said, "Sinners are often most secure when they are most in danger and destruction is at the door."

With a false sense of security, Nabal partied hard, but morning inevitably came. And with the dawning of a new day, Abigail confronted her husband. She did not discuss the previous night's imprudent actions, and she did not mention what he should have done—that would be using a hands-on methodology. Instead, Abigail relied on God's oversight as she informed Nabal what happened after he discarded David's request for rations.

God's hand simultaneously controlled her household and Nabal's mortality. He is a perfect example of a man with a cold, hardened heart. It is possible to misinterpret his *heart* as the organ that pumps blood. The Hebrew word for heart in this passage is defined as the soul, conscious, and the seat of emotions, passions, and courage. Though his blood pumped Nabal was mentally, emotionally, and spiritually dead. According to 1 Samuel 25:38, "About ten days later, the Lord struck Nabal and he died."

After Hannah gave birth to Samuel and weaned him from her breast, she kept her word and gave her boy to Eli, the priest, to serve the Lord the rest of his days. 1 Samuel 2:1-10 quotes her prayer with verse six saying, "The Lord brings death and makes alive; he brings down to the grave and raises up." God is the author of life and death, so He ordered Nabal's demise.

When we trust that He is a hands-on God, we do not need to wring our hands in wonder or worry over our tomorrows. Place your household in God's hands and take your hands off what you asked Him to touch.

KEY POINT: FOLLOWERS OF JESUS POSSESS FOLLOW THROUGH

If we are not careful, we can misread the love stories in God's Word like we read romance novels or watch soap operas and trendy network dramas. Too many Christian women are influenced by fictitious drama, and it blurs the reality and intention of Biblical stories.

Abigail's story is Hollywood and romance-writer worthy, but God intended for it to be purposeful and to point to Him. When David heard about Nabal's death, he praised God for faithfully being hands-on in a provoking situation. David also recognized it was God who intervened and kept David's hands off Nabal.

As followers of Jesus we must complete follow-through. Acting premature, walking off God's straight path, picking and choosing which statutes to obey, or altering His commands are not following Him all the way through a situation.

Imagine if Jesus dropped His cross and walked away. What if the blood of Jesus only covered 98 percent of humanity's sin? It is absurd to consider. Jesus gave His all, and like the old hymn "Jesus Paid it All" declares, so all to Him we owe.

God was not done ordering Abigail's steps. If she faithfully followed Him, her next steps would be revealed. In 1 Samuel 25:39-40, David sent his servants to Abigail asking her to become his wife. David was captivated by her character and conduct. If she could be a good wife to Nabal, the fool, then David believed Abigail would be a good fit for him. After all, she accepted his anointing and respected his authority as future king. So, David graciously pursued her.

KEY POINT: DISPLAY A SERVANT'S HEART

Every spouse has those few things they would rather not do. For me, I would prefer not to take out the garbage, wash windows, or do yardwork. These are a few of my least favorite things. For Kevin, it is grocery shopping, calling the mechanic, and preparing meals. So, imagine my delight when my beloved offered to go to the grocery store with me. It gets better. He knew I needed more time to write, so he suggested I go to our summer place, and he would stay home with our two teens and *prepare meals*. I am married to a man with a servant's heart. (He washes windows, too.) We can have a servant's heart, but evidencing it takes it to another level. A previous key point emphasized being selfless. Displaying a servant's heart will confirm selflessness.

David's servants were authorized to go to Abigail and deliver his proposal. Abigail was not compelled through rank or position to say yes. Her response to David was her choice.

1 Samuel 25:41-42 recounts her noble response:

- She bowed down *"with her face to the ground, she says..."*

- She offered herself *"here is your maidservant..."*

- She was ready to serve *"ready to serve you..."*

- She was prepared to serve *"and wash the feet of my master's servants."*

She spoke the part, looked the part, promised the part, and acted the part of a true servant. I wonder what the servants were thinking when she said she was willing to wash their dirty feet. This woman had lived with a surly and mean man; foul feet were more inviting than dealing with a fool. A servant heart isn't deterred by what's disgusting and dirty. Sacrifice and unconditional love should motivate us to fight for our household.

KEY POINT: BE READY TO PRESS ON

Have you noticed things do not always land as you had planned or expected? Fallout from difficult circumstances can have the capacity to derail, delude, or disappoint. When Jesus carries us through, what appears to be the end is not necessarily final because we are not responsible for the results.

In 2 Corinthians Paul encourages believers and teaches how we fight through turbulent times and manage the aftermath before it comes, as it rages, and through the wreckage. Paul's encouragement is that we should have our attention on what we cannot see because it has eternal reward. Before Paul tells us where to look, he says, "For our light and momentary troubles are achieving for us an eternal glory that far outweighs them all." (2 Corinthians 4:17)

Paul continues. 2 Corinthians 4:18 says, "So we fix our eyes not on what is seen, but on what is unseen." A passage I often use as I speak and write says, "Let us fix our eyes on Jesus…" (Hebrews 12:2) *Fix* is one word in English, but two different words in Greek.

In the Hebrews verse the word has a two-step process for its meaning. We must look away from what has our attention, and then we can adhere our gaze on Jesus. The implication is we cannot have our eyes in two directions. The word for fix in 2 Corinthians 4:18 means to observe, contemplate, and direct your attention to.

My husband and I often say, "Whatever has your attention has you." If Abigail's momentary afflictions— Nabal and the threat on her household—had her attention, her home would have been in shambles. We must fight right for our households—focused on what we cannot see: the eternal glory that Paul wrote of and God promised. (2 Corinthians 4:17)

Paul wrote of another reinforcement found in Philippians 3:12-14. Portions read, "...I press on to take hold of that which Christ Jesus took hold of me...one thing I do: Forgetting what is behind and straining toward what is ahead, I press on toward the goal..."

Contrary to popular opinion, we are not designed to multi-task. And we are not able to have our complete attention in two directions. A runner has one aim – to finish. And in a race there is only one finish line. Paul urges followers of Jesus to eagerly and earnestly seek the final prize—our heavenly reward for bearing Christ-like character.

All too often we are focused on what we are not getting, receiving, or accomplishing as we struggle through hard times. Fighting right does not focus on what we gain now. Followers of Jesus who fight for the things worth fighting for fight through any and all hardships knowing our eternal reward is already set.

Abigail could press on because she pressed in to God. She entrusted all her tomorrows to Him. We, too, should tuck in tight to Jesus and press on. When Paul says we are to forget what is behind, it means to no longer care, to stop giving attention to it. Our relationship with God is like a race—if we leave the starting block looking backwards, we will trip and fall.

PONDER
deeply, carefully, and thoughtfully consider

1. Consider the foundation of your household. What is it? Are there cracks? Is it sturdy? What changes need to be made so it will not crumble and fall?

2. Carefully consider what key points from this chapter are you challenged with regarding your household?

PERSUADE
God's Word influences, encourages, and guides

1. Read Proverbs 1:3. A disciplined life requires prudence. With 1 being low and 5 being high, rank how you do in matters involving your household. Then, in your own words, write the definition of each word.

_____ wise:

_____ sagacious:

_____ sober:

_____ discreet:

_____ mindful:

2. 1 Samuel 25:41-42 recounts Abigail's noble response. How does Abigail model servanthood?

3. Walking with the Lord is an everyday choice. Write out how Deuteronomy 11:18-20 influences your walk with the Lord in your household.

PRACTICAL
applying Biblical Truth to present day

1. If *whatever has your attention has you* is true, what in your household has your attention?

   According to the following passages, how can God's Word help you have proper perspective?

   Hebrews 12:2

   2 Corinthians 4:18

   Philippians 3:12-14

   Proverbs 12:25

   Psalm 63:8

2. How can Joshua 24:14-15 be applied to your household?

PERSONAL
inviting Jesus into your current reality

1. Describe the difference between confronting and being confrontational. Which better describes you? Write out a *confrontation plan* for your household.

2. Tension is a part of a household. How does your household avoid dissension?

5

be ready to fight WISE

"Do not be wise in your own eyes..."
Proverbs 3:7

As one of three girls raised by Allen and Linda, I am grateful for my upbringing. In the late 1960s and 1970s, Dad and Mom sheltered us from a few popular television shows. That does not mean we always obeyed, since I remember watching random episodes of some of the prohibited programs. *The Three Stooges* was on the list of the forbidden. I am sure it was more Mom's judgement than Dad's. I think she thought if her girls watched the slapstick comedy, we would be poking eyes out, slapping foreheads, and playing pranks.

A recent internet search brought me to a short video featuring Larry, Curly, Moe, and Shemp. The one minute and thirty-five second compilation uses forty-one different clips of the famous comedians repeating the infamous phrase, "Oh, a wise guy, eh?" Without guilt, I laughed.

It is not a compliment to be called a wise guy. The

term refers to one who is obnoxiously conceited, cocky, and insolent. These are not useful traits when fighting for the things worth fighting for. However, a wise man or woman is ready to fight right. Dictionary.com defines wise as having the power to discern and judge properly what is true or right. A wise person is judicious based on fact, not feeling, and concerned with truth rather than opinion.

We can call someone wise, but according to Proverbs 9:10, "The fear of the Lord is the beginning of wisdom..." Therefore, they are only wise if they first fear God.

KEY POINT: SLOW LIVING, IS WISE LIVING

SLOW livin' is a mantra of mine and a common theme in my writing and teaching. Years ago I was studying what it means to fear the Lord. Deuteronomy 10:12-13, revealed the answer. "...what does the Lord require of you, but to fear the Lord your God, to **walk** in all his ways, to **love** him, to **serve** the Lord your God with all your heart and with all your soul, and to **observe** the Lord's commands and decrees...for your own good." (bold and italics, mine)

Because memorization is not a strong suit of mine, I rearranged the four emphasized verbs, creating the acronym, SLOW:

Serve God

Love God

Observe His commands

Walk in all His ways

Are you aware how many times this word is used on roadside signs, painted on blacktopped parking lots, posted on billboards, or on a sign held by a road crew worker? Since 2009, God has used this four-letter expression often to remind, reprimand, even rebuke my off-kilter behavior, attitude, or mindset.

According to the last four words in the Deuteronomy passage, it is *for your own good* to fear the Lord. To fight right we need God's wisdom; therefore, we need to pray He will send a SLOW living man or woman to counsel us as we fight for the things worth fighting for.

In 2 Samuel 14:2, 17:19, and 20:16, we meet three different SLOW living women. They are nameless, yet remarkable; unfamiliar, still influential. Before we meet these wise women and identify their instrumental roles, we need to broaden our scope of the narrative.

In 2 Samuel, chapter eleven, we find the well-known Bible story of David and Bathsheba. For years, David had been Israel's king. Back in 1 Samuel 13:14, the prophet Samuel referred to David as a man after God's own heart. However, in the eleventh chapter of 2 Samuel, King David defies this description.

Condensing the story, David should have been with his army, fighting for his kingdom. Instead, he chose to remain in the palace. One night he was on the roof and saw a woman bathing. (The woman was Bathsheba, the wife of Uriah, one of the king's royal guards.) David lingered and lust took over. David demanded she be brought to him. He slept with her, and she became pregnant. David then orchestrated an elaborate cover-up scheme that involved the calculated murder of her husband and the unnecessary deaths of other men.

In the twelfth chapter of 2 Samuel the Lord sends Nathan to David. Nathan was a wise man and confronted

David regarding his sinful ways. He repented. God redeemed and restored David who is known as a man after God's own heart.

KEY POINT: GUILT IS GONE, RAMIFICATIONS REMAIN

God's Word is clear. Repented sin is removed from our record. Psalm 103:11-12 says, "...so great is his love for those who *fear him*; as far as the east is from the west, so far has he removed our transgressions from us." Imagine guilt being attached to a transgression. When God accepts true repentance, He removes all guilt. If you struggle with guilt, perhaps it's because you're still hanging on to something God threw into oblivion. Being under the shroud of guilt keeps us from seeing and accepting the consequences that remain.

Speaking for God, Nathan's words cut David's heart. (2 Samuel 12:1-12) The reprimand reminded David he was God's anointed man and that God rescued and provided for him when Saul wanted him dead. The reproof confronted the affair and the murder and communicated the consequences.

"Now, therefore," Nathan said, "The sword will never depart from your house." (2 Samuel 12:10) He continued, "Out of your own household I am going to bring calamity upon you. Before your very eyes I will take your wives and give them to one who is close to you, and he will lie with your wives in broad daylight. You did it in secret, but I will do this thing in broad daylight before all Israel." (2 Samuel 12:11-12)

Then David repented. "I have sinned against the Lord."

And Nathan responded, "The Lord has taken away your sin." David, your guilt is gone.

In 2 Samuel 12:14, Nathan continued, "But…" David was about to learn the ramifications remained. Nathan went on to describe what the consequence would be. Though David fasted and agonized in prayer for grace and mercy, when the consequence came, he accepted it— without question or doubt in the sovereignty or providence of God.

In the course of time, the calamity Nathan had spoken of raged into David's household. Despicable acts of abuse, murder, cover up, conspiracy, manipulation, sexual depravity, and public perversion erupted within the bloodline. Only God's wisdom can break through the complexities of corruption.

Followers of Jesus get stuck on their faith journey when they avoid the reality that ramifications are a part of the journey. They get misled when they perceive the consequence as bigger than God's grace. Like David, we need a Nathan. We need a God-fearing person to speak truth and wisdom into our lives.

KEY POINT: WISE MAY BE WILY

Most are familiar with Wile E. Coyote. It's obvious the cartoon character's first name is a pun since Mr. Coyote constantly strategizes how to entice the Road Runner and catch him. Wile E. orders gadgets to assist in the capture, but the plan always turns, and the wily creature fails at getting his intended meal. Wise may be wily, but wily is not always wise.

Years separate 2 Samuel 12 and 2 Samuel 14. During that time, one of David's sons successfully sought another son's demise. After he killed Amnon Absalom fled the kingdom. Three years later a wise woman is called upon by Joab, a commander in the king's army, to play a key role in the plan to return Absalom to the king.

The Hebrew word for wise is chakam (pronounced khaw-kawm) and has many meanings. Three wise women will highlight six different character traits defining the word *chakam*. God used these women to fight right and impart wisdom for the saving and rescuing of lives linked to David's sin with Bathsheba and his depraved and elaborate cover-ups that caused upheaval and mayhem within his family and negatively affected his kingdom. The first wise woman was wily. The second woman highlights how being shrewd and subtle can be wise. And the third woman characterizes how clever, crafty, and cunning were used for good.

To wile means to beguile; to mislead or delude. At face value wily does not appear wise. Joab knew the king mourned one son's death, but David also had another son missing in action. Joab's first concern was for the safety of the kingdom. But he also knew the dispute between King David and Absalom, who was next in line to the throne, was a complication. To fight right, Joab, called on the wiles of a capable female conspirator who creatively adapted his stratagem.

Introducing Wise Woman #1
2 Samuel 14:2

2 Samuel 14:2 says, "And Joab sent to Tekoa, and fetched thence a wise woman…" (King James Version) It is unclear if she was willing, but after she was fetched, throughout the account, she was unquestionably wily. Like a stage performance, Joab directed the woman to pretend she was in mourning and act like she had spent days grieving for the dead. The plan was to confront the king and play a role with *the moral of the story* type of ending. So the woman dressed the part and gave her award-winning, wily

performance.

After she fell at the king's feet, David asked what was troubling her. The monologue confirmed recent widowhood and how her two sons had fought in a field and one son killed the other. She told of an uprising in her clan demanding she hand over the guilty son so he could be put to death. The act continued as she pled for her son's life claiming he was the only left to carry on her deceased husband's name.

After the king granted absolution for her son, the wise woman challenged the king. Referring to the exile of Absalom, David's son who was missing in action after he killed his brother, she asked why the king had done the same thing against God's people. David knew Joab was behind the performance and yielded to the wise man's advice. A wise woman's wily actions helped King David fight right for his family.

I remember the first time I helped a woman who was being abused by her husband. Marriage is God's idea; therefore, it is worth fighting for. But it also requires godly wisdom. I am all about coming alongside a hurting wife and fighting for her marriage. But when I am aware a woman is in an abusive marriage, I will fight for what is right and keep her safe.

As outsiders received his kindness, she got his wrath. He built others up but tore her down. Verbally, he attacked. Physically, he knew where to push or punch so the bruises could be hidden. One day she told me the truth, so we immediately moved her to a safe location. I received phone calls and texts from her husband demanding her whereabouts. Her reality required wise responses. His abusive nature warranted wily intervention.

KEY POINT: WISDOM NEVER RUNS DRY

There have been times when others share their heavy burdens and I think, "I have nothing to give." However, the good news for God's children is our Father has a never-ending storehouse of wisdom, and He is willing to impart what we need.

James 1:5 says, "If any of you lacks wisdom, he should ask God, who gives generously…" James knew the human condition. Perhaps he struggled with a lack of wisdom and experienced doubt. In verses six and seven, he goes on to say, "But when he asks, he must believe and not doubt, because he is like a wave of the sea, blown and tossed by the wind. That man should not think he will receive anything from the Lord; he is a double-minded man, unstable in all he does."

Five words immediately stand out when I read this passage. *That man should not think*. Of course, God is also speaking to women. It is not necessary to get in a huff over the use of male nouns and pronouns. This issue is not a fight worth fighting for. If you are a female, just apply it; do not fight it.

When I think *I have nothing to give* from the wisdom department, it's because I am thinking and not asking. James says to ask for wisdom and God will generously or lavishly give it to us, meaning He will simply, openly, frankly, and sincerely impart His wisdom.

James was adamant. As we ask we do so in faith, believing that God will do what He says He will do. When we doubt, we waver and hesitate. That is the ironic thing about the wily coyote, he never hesitated or doubted he could get the Road Runner.

When lacking wisdom go to God. He will provide the right strategy and the means to carry it out and to fight right.

The wisdom from the wily woman in 2 Samuel 14,

accomplished what Joab was hoping for—he brought Absalom back to Jerusalem. But the king's son did not return for a family reunion; he turned to his conniving and manipulative ways. He was set on overtaking his father's throne and he would stop at nothing to get what he wanted:

- He stole the hearts of the men of Israel. 2 Samuel 15:6

- He lied to his father, King David. 2 Samuel 15:8

- He sent secret messengers for personal gain. 2 Samuel 15:10

- He swayed David's men to follow him. 2 Samuel 15:11

- His conspiracy gained strength. 2 Samuel 15:12

David has a kingdom, a home, and a family to protect. To fight right he needs wisdom! When the messenger came to David with news of Absalom's conspiracy, the king fled with his entire household and with many people following him. But he left ten concubines to take care of the palace. (2 Samuel 15:16)

David was a mighty warrior. As a shepherd he fought bears that attacked his flocks. As a teen boy he bravely and boldly faced a giant that intimidated the entire Israel army, and he took the Philistine down with his slingshot and one smooth stone. David went toe-to-toe with massive armies; he fought in many battles; he planned attacks and led victory marches. This king knew how to fight.

Sometimes backing down is fighting right. In 2 Samuel 15, though it may appear King David had lost courage, he was really acting wise. He remembered God's word to him through Nathan. The consequences told to David after he repented of his sin with Bathsheba were in play. David was wise to remember the ramifications.

Hasn't David lost enough? He learned his lesson, right? Why would God make Absalom rebel? If God was a loving God, He would stop this whole travesty. It is not right that David must leave his kingdom.

The retorts vary and are many. Wise followers of Jesus accept there are consequences for disobedience. Wise followers stop retorting and completely trust all God's ways. And wise followers remain tucked in tight to Jesus, confident that all they see, know, and experience is first filtered through the fingers of God.

KEY POINT: WHEN EXHAUSTED, THE WISE ARE REFRESHED

In 2 Samuel 16:2, God provides "...donkeys...to ride on, bread and fruit...to eat, and wine to refresh those who become exhausted in the desert." Along our faith journey God allows dark, dry, and dreary experiences, difficult and confusing times. Bad memories surface. Loneliness, desperation, and hopelessness threaten.

Proverbs 24:14 promises, "Know also that wisdom is sweet to your soul; if you find it, there is a future hope for you, and your hope will not be cut off."

Proverbs 4:6 sustains us through hard times. "Do not forget wisdom, and she will protect you; love her, and she will watch over you." David remembered wisdom. David wisely tucked in tight to God and he was protected in practical and surprising ways.

2 Samuel 16:5-14 tells of a certain man who verbally cursed David and pelted his men with stones as they passed through a town. One of David's men courageously honored the king by asking for permission to cut the head off the cursing man. But David would not allow it. The wise king said, "Leave him alone..." Though David had the authority and the ability to subdue, and even kill, the cursing man, he chose wisdom over convention or vengeance. David experienced what happened when he impulsively reacted versus when he responded the right way. Reactions are not wise. Wise responses come from God.

HALT is an acronym used as a mental health principle to describe when we are most vulnerable to making poor decisions or reacting instead of responding right. David and his men were **H**ungry, **A**ngry, **L**onely and **T**ired, but David wisely responded. Wisdom inspires us to turn the other cheek. We must be wise and relent to the providence of God.

Proverbs 14:33 says wisdom is at home and at rest in an understanding heart. Peace and quiet came to David even as the man continued to curse.

Exhausted, David and his men needed refreshment. 2 Samuel 16:14 says, "...all the people...arrived...exhausted. And there he refreshed himself." The original word used for *refreshed* means to take a breath. David is satisfied by the bread and the wine refreshment he received earlier.

Whenever we take communion the bread and the cup symbolize the body and blood of Jesus. He told His disciples to take, eat, and drink often. As we remember His sacrifice, we are satisfied and refreshed for our faith journey.

KEY POINT: WISE PEOPLE, WAIT WELL

In 2 Samuel 16:15-17:14, Absalom received the advice of his trusted advisor regarding a plan of attack on David and his men. Absalom took the advice to a different advisor to sanction the plan. But the second advisor, Hushai, nullified the idea and proposed a better plan. And Absalom endorsed it.

Meanwhile, David waited to hear from God or to see His hand move. 2 Samuel 17:13 describes, "For the Lord had determined to frustrate the advice of [the first advisor] in order to bring disaster on Absalom." David wisely waited and trusted God.

If we interrupt God we will miss part of His plan. If we are not tucked in tight to Jesus, we will not be ready when He calls us to participate in a worthy fight. Hushai told two priests "(The other advisor) advised Absalom to do such and such, but I have advised them to do so and so…" (2 Samuel 17:15) Let us make sure we have this correct; the *such and such* plan will flop, while the *so and so* plan will succeed. Yes, that is right.

Hushai called for messengers to get word to David to keep moving through the desert and cross over the Jordan River, to move further away from Absalom's impending barrage. But according to 2 Samuel 17:18, a young man saw the messengers and told Absalom, who assumed they were on their way to David. So they quickly left and went to the house of another man in a nearby city. When they arrived in his courtyard, they noticed a well and climbed down into it to hide from Absalom and his men.

Introducing Wise Woman #2
2 Samuel 17:19

On our best day we cannot compete with God's rescue plan. Psalm 91:14-15 says, "Because he loves me,' says the Lord, 'I will rescue him; I will protect him, for he acknowledges my name...I will be with him in trouble, I will deliver him...'" We spend a lot of time trying to help an Omnipotent God and question His omniscience.

When we are facing difficulty, if we wisely trust God, we will fully experience His faithfulness and accept our current reality. (Sometimes, His rescue plan for us is to rescue us from ourselves.) If we are willing to take our eyes off our issues and wisely ask Him to use us, however He sees fit, He may use us to participate in another person's rescue operation.

My friend and mentor, Beth, taught me the value and power of praying two words. *Jesus, come* can be applied to many situations and circumstances. It can end with a comma, ellipsis, period, or exclamation point, but never a question mark. It can even be prayed as we are on the move.

Though she's not referred to as wise, 2 Samuel 17:19 tells of a woman who acted wise without a moment's notice, with no time to scheme. We may face a fight and not have time to call or text a prayer partner. But because God is omnipresent, a breath prayer suffices when a situation warrants immediate action.

KEY POINT: WISE MAY BE SHREWD

The wise woman in 2 Samuel 17:19 was shrewd— astute and sharp in practical matters. Like Abigail, she was sagacious. She saw the men climb into the well and, without missing a beat, she took a covering, spread it over the opening, and scattered grain over it to appear like ground cover. The verse ends by saying, "No one knew anything about it." Quick thinking must be judiciously wise. God planted the idea and she astutely went with it.

Years ago, Kevin and I went to his seminary alma mater to attend a pastor's conference. We made plans to stay twenty-five minutes away. On the second day of the conference, we awoke to huge snowflakes falling from the sky and a blanket of fresh snow on the ground.

Asbury Theological Seminary is in Kentucky. Snow falls, so the hilly roads and winding curves make it difficult to maneuver. Kevin and I knew we needed to think fast: get to the seminary before the roads were impassable. On the way we were stopped at a red light on an incline. As the light turned green, the brake lights remained red on the vehicle in front of us. Every time the driver took her foot off the brake, she slid backwards. Impatient drivers behind us blared their horns.

I got out of our vehicle, walked to the car in front of us, opened the driver's door and said, "I'm from Michigan..." (Obviously, I thought that explained my next move.) Her look of shock showed a bit of gratefulness, but there was something else in her eyes. I did not take time to inquire. I continued, "...get out, let me drive." Perplexed, she responded to my order and got out. Noticing it was a stick-shift, I engaged the clutch, operated the brake and accelerator, and moved her vehicle up the incline. As I put the emergency brake on, I looked in the rearview mirror to see if Kevin was making it up the hill and noticed a baby in the back seat of the vehicle that I had just ordered the mother to vacate. That explained the look in her eyes. The experience called for shrewdness, not subtlety.

KEY POINT: WISE MAY BE SUBTLE

After the wise woman spread the grain on the covering hiding the opening to the well, Absalom's men came to her and inquired about the men who were seen running in her direction. Without missing another beat she answered, "They crossed over the brook." (2 Samuel 17:20) The men searched but found no one so they returned to Jerusalem. All because one quick-thinking, wise woman subtly pointed the men in a different direction.

She had nothing to gain, but everything to lose. And yet, she jumped at the chance to help. Only the Spirit of God can nudge a heart and a mind and a body to action in a split second. Her shrewdness is noted within just two verses of Scripture. In my Bible her starring role is captured in 64 words. A small story, but one significant act of wisdom.

This woman could not act with wisdom if the Spirit of God was not involved. The men asked their question and she responded. Mental acuteness is necessary when making split-second decisions. Subtlety is wise in moments of quick thinking. Subtlety requires a mind transformed and consecrated for the Lord's purposes.

The remaining portion of Chapter 17, and following through Chapter 19 of 2 Samuel, chronicles Absalom's death that left King David mourning the loss of another son. It also tells how Commander Joab confronted the king and reminded him that his family, his household, his kingdom, his men and their families were all saved from the wake of Absalom's great harm, bloodshed, and evil. Joab encouraged his king to do the right thing and lead well.

The old hymn "Take My Life, And Let It Be" was written by Frances Havergal. One time Frances went to visit ten people in one home. In her words, "…some were unconverted and long prayed for, some converted but not rejoicing Christians." She prayed, *Lord, give me all in this house.* And He did. Every person was saved and filled with the Holy Spirit! Frances was so excited and overwhelmed she stayed up most of the night. She described the late hours with God as, "…in renewal of my consecration."

STAND ready / Ellen Harbin

Consecration simply means to be set apart and used by God for His purposes. Frances was set apart and used mightily in one evening. According to Frances, "Ever only, all for Thee!" Too many followers of Jesus apply a subtle change to her lyric making it *Take my life; but let me be.* Wise Christians allow God to make the necessary changes in their life so they can be used ever only all for Thee. Using Frances' paraphrased lyrics, what needs to be consecrated in your life?

> Your moments and your days, so they flow in ceaseless praise?
>
> Your hands, so they move, at the impulse of God's love?
>
> Your feet, so they're swift and beautiful?
>
> Your voice, to sing, always, only, for your King?
>
> Your lips, so they're filled with messages from God?
>
> Your silver and gold; withholding nothing?
>
> Your intellect, so God can choose to use every power?
>
> Your will, so it becomes God's, no longer yours?
>
> Your heart, so it will be the throne where Jesus dwells?
>
> Your love; poured and stored at the feet of Jesus?

Frances Havergal and a subtly wise woman from God's Word lived consecrated for the Lord. They lived *ever only, all for Thee.*

God uses followers of Jesus in His story. Are you like this wise woman, willing and available to join God where He

is already at work? Or have you missed being used in His story, with many opportunities long gone? It is not too late to get on board when God calls as the Holy Spirit stirs you to action.

KEY POINT: BE INFLUENCED, NOT IMPRESSED

There was such an uprising in Israel and Judah chaos and confusion reigned. King David took heed of Joab's wise counsel and returned to Jerusalem. Sometimes there are pauses between trouble. But King David encountered another problem—a troublemaker named Sheba had routed the men of Israel to join his rebellion against Judah. (2 Samuel 20)

Sheba used impressive angles to gain followers. He was loud drawing attention to his cause. And like a politician whose campaign ads have negative talk about the opponent, instead of letting his constituents know what he can do for them, Sheba crusaded the Israelites to join him. Sheba was out to impress men.

However, David was wise; he used influence. The king returned to his home. The first thing he did was remove the ten concubines he had left to oversee the palace. He had them put in a house under guard and kept them in confinement, living as widows the rest of their lives. (2 Samuel 20:3)

King David did not kick ten women out of his palace; he removed a representation of past sin. He knew their presence was a stumbling block to righteousness within the palace. So he wisely put his past under guard so it could not come back and threaten his relationship with God and harm his household.

Proverbs 24:3 says, "By wisdom a house is built, and through understanding it is established; through knowledge its rooms are filled with rare and beautiful treasures." If things from the past are disrupting your relationship with Jesus, then there is no room for the rare and beautiful treasures God desires to give you. Be wise. Put those past interruptions under guard, lock them up tight, and hand the key over to God.

We need to follow David's example. If we are to live ever only all for Thee, we need to wisely remove things from our past that have us stumbling on our faith journey, disrupting our households, and keeping us from holy living.

David continued to influence his household and lead his kingdom with wisdom. In 2 Samuel 20:4-15, his men followed the king's order to pursue Sheba because of the potential for mass destruction in Judah. David's army strategized for battle. They besieged Sheba, closed in on his troops, and readied themselves for attack. At Joab's command the warriors began battering down the city walls. Suddenly, they were interrupted by hollering.

Introducing Wise Woman #3
2 Samuel 20:16-22

KEY POINT: WISE IS CLEVER, CRAFTY, CUNNING

Not all interruptions are bad. At times I interrupt Kevin in conversation. Thoughts come and they quickly turn to words. Impulsivity interrupts. Wisdom interjects. The hollering that stopped David's men came from an interjecting woman.

Some may call her crazy, but God calls her wise. Joab, probably stained in blood from an earlier confrontation, along with all the mighty warriors determined to wage war on a troublemaker, was fiercely hammering down a wall when a woman yelled up to them.

She is my kind of woman! Boisterous, daring, and unintimidated. Add wise to the package and she is unstoppable—inspiring and motivating to fight right for the things worth fighting for. The Hebrew word for wise includes clever, crafty, and cunning.

CLEVER

This woman is sharp and inventive. She loudly proclaimed, "Hear, hear!" (We say, "Listen up!") Warriors recognized a battle cry, and they knew their commander's voice. A female shouting in their direction and giving orders was not familiar to these men. And yet, it caught their attention and stopped their demolition. "...Tell Joab to come here so I can speak to him."

2 Samuel 20:17 records, "He went toward her..." God's hand obviously maneuvered everyone. Like pieces on a chessboard to fight the way God orchestrated, He positioned each player where they needed to be.

She asked, "Are you Joab?"

"I am," he answered.

She said, "Listen to what your servant has to say."

"I'm listening," he said.

In 2 Samuel 20:18-19, this wise, ingenious woman spoke. She told Joab her city was known for sharing wise advice. People used to come there to settle disputes. Each side would share, and each side would listen, agreeing to walk away. She cannot imagine this place of peace being in ruins.

CRAFTY

Motivation and purpose matter. Proverbs 17:24 says, "A discerning man keeps wisdom in view..." If we are motivated by wisdom, we will fight right. If we are guided by wisdom, crafty will be purposeful and not used for selfish gain. Defined, crafty is skillful in underhand schemes. However, a good and honest salesman guided by wisdom can be crafty. At time managers and executives wisely use craftiness to lead their teams well.

The wise woman continued, "We are the peaceful and faithful in Israel." (We serve a faithful God; He will always position a remnant of faithful followers.) Being a wise communicator, she crafted a powerful statement and posed a challenging question. "You are trying to destroy a city…why do you want to swallow up the Lord's inheritance." (2 Samuel 20:19)

Her wise words snapped Joab to attention. "Far be it from me to swallow up or destroy! That is not the case." He went on to let her know they were after one man, Sheba, and he was hiding in her city. He offered his terms, "Hand over this one man, and I'll withdraw from the city."

This woman was not done fighting for her people. She would not stop until all harm was gone. She would not quit until peace reigned.

CUNNING

Currently, Kevin and I are parenting two teenagers. In 2002 our oldest child turned thirteen. For seventeen years we have had teenagers in our home. For seventeen years we engaged in many fights regarding things worth fighting for. But we did not always fight right.

Today, our youngest is fourteen. We have four more years of frontline, active-duty parenting years left. We have never given up on any of our six kids, and we never will. Therefore, it is imperative Kevin and I remain ready to fight right and not just engage in battle.

All parents need wisdom. All parents need to wisely fight. When it comes to parenting, sometimes *desperate times call for desperate measures*. It can also be said, *fighting times, call for cunning actions*.

Wise parenting is used for shock value. *Son, if you talk back to me one more time, I may ram you up against that wall.* Shock value. *Honey, lock your bedroom door on me again, and the door comes down.* Shock value. My son was shocked when I tackled him into the wall in front of his friend. My daughter was equally shocked when she returned home to her door-less bedroom.

Ingenuity is cleverly inventive and resourceful. Cunning is artfully sly proving ingenuity. Again, motive and purpose matter. In 2 Samuel 20:19 we see a wise woman respond to Joab's terms. "The woman said to Joab, 'His head will be thrown to you from the wall."

2 Samuel 20:22 goes on, "Then the woman went to all the people with her **wise advice**, and they cut off the head of Sheba…and threw it to Joab. So, he sounded the trumpet and his men dispersed from the city…and Joab went back to the king…"

Talk about shock! At times, God's ways may be surprising and alarming. Ask Jonah who spent three nights in the belly of a big fish. Or Daniel, who was thrown into a burning furnace and a den of lions. Ask Samson about the honey God provided in the carcass of a lion. We may struggle to comprehend how or why God acts or allows certain situations. The question is are you going to allow the shocking moments to hinder you from participating in God's plan? If yes, you are not walking in full obedience to where He is leading.

Proverbs 21:30 says, "There is no wisdom, no insight, no plan that can succeed against the Lord." There are many things fighting against the things worth fighting for—families, marriage, sobriety, the church, truth, purity, freedom, friendships, and so much more! We must tuck in tight to Jesus, abide in Him, follow Him faithfully, walk in complete obedience to God's Word, and fear God to be ready for the holy alarms and surprises God allows if we are ready to fight right.

If this were a fiction narrative and we wanted the reader to grasp the moral of the story, it could be said *troublemakers lose their heads; don't be a troublemaker.* God's Word is not fiction; it is alive and active and sharper than any two-edged sword.

So, what wisdom can we glean from this true story? How can we apply the demise of a headless troublemaker to our lives today? The Hebrew definition for *cut off* means to cut, cut down, eliminate, and kill:

1. Cut off what keeps you from living peaceably.

2. Cut down what is in the way of your relationship with Jesus.

3. Eliminate what threatens your household.

4. Kill the lies, the deceit, the pride, the anger, the doubt, the anxiety, the fear—anything that rears its ugly head of trouble—cut it out of your life!

To fight right for the things worth fighting for, we must stand ready and wise.

PONDER

deeply, carefully, and thoughtfully consider

1. What is **SLOW** livin'? (Deuteronomy 10:12-13)   To be ready to fight wise, write in the box which part of **SLOW** needs to be fully surrendered?

S __ __ __ __ God

L __ __ __ God

O __ __ __ __ __ __ His commands

W __ __ __ in all His ways

2. We unwisely allow/invite/welcome guilt and shame into our life instead of understanding the reality that ramifications are a part of our faith journey. How has this affected your walk with Jesus?

PERSUADE
God's Word influences, encourages, and guides

1. Use James 1:5-8 to answer the following questions.

    v. 5 - What do we lack?

    v. 5 - How can get what we lack?

    v 6 - What stops us from asking?

    v 6 - What are we like when we doubt?

    v 7 - What gets in the way?

    v 8 - If we do not believe that God will give us the wisdom we lack, what are we?

2. Read Proverbs 21:30 and Proverbs 24:14.
   How do these verses

    ...influence you to be wise?

    ...encourage you to be wise?

    ...guide you to be wise?

PRACTICAL
applying Biblical Truth to present day

1. Looking back at 2 Samuel 20.
   We met Sheba, the troublemaker. (vs. 1)

   How can you wisely respond to the troublemakers in your life?

   David put a representation of his past under guard. (vs. 3) What needs to be wisely locked up or kept under guard in your life?

2. Read the following verses about wisdom.
   How can you apply the wise advice to your life?

   Proverbs 24:3

   Proverbs 17:24

   Proverbs 14:33

PERSONAL
inviting Jesus into your current reality

1. In your own words, give a useful definition and one example of how these six types of wisdom can benefit your current reality.

WILY _____

_____

_____

SHREWD_____

_____

_____

SUBTLE _____

_____

_____

CLEVER_____

_____

_____

CRAFTY _____

_____

_____

CUNNING _____

_____

_____

6

be ready to fight when EMPTY

"Blessed are those who hunger and thirst for
righteousness, for they will be filled."
Matthew 5:6

At our summer place a jar sits on the counter with one purpose: it contains M&M's. For me a serving is one of each color. I do not visit the jar often, but when I do I expect a rainbow of chocolatey goodness to satisfy any spontaneous, yet infrequent, craving.

Not long ago I went to our place to work on this book. I was settled in ready to study and write. I had a hankering for the multi-colored morsels. They are like fuel for the journey and inspiration for the task at hand. Expectantly, I went to the jar with a double portion on my mind.

Empty! The jar was empty! Who was to blame? Since my son and his wife were the last occupants, it did not take a lengthy investigation to figure out who emptied the contents. (Good thing I had a secret stash!)

Empty is an adjective and a verb. It describes when something contains nothing or is vacant and it means the act of depriving or discharging contents. An empty candy jar is nothing compared to bare cupboards or an unfilled refrigerator.

There are many opinions regarding beggars at intersections. A news outlet in one community we lived near reported on a man pretending to be homeless and hungry, taking in hundreds of dollars per week from his panhandling sham. Regardless, many people legitimately beg. The reasons vary, but the need is the same.

A couple of years ago my two youngest kids and I were on our way home. I'm not sure why, but a stash of granola bars was in the minivan. As we approached the stoplight, I could see the man standing on the corner, cardboard sign in hand.

"Jaylen fetch me that box of granola bars," I said.

"Why momma? Sukanya asked.

Jaylen responded first, "Because that man needs them."

I opened the window and gave the man the granola bars. Honestly, my motive was to teach my kids a lesson more than to help the man. We drove away, but the instruction continued with the vehicle our classroom. After all, something taught must get caught. Though we would have enjoyed the granola bars, we had an opportunity to make a small deposit into another person's emptiness.

KEY POINT: A DROUGHT FROM GOD IS A WAKE-UP CALL

1 Kings 17:1 begins with Elijah confronting King Ahab with news that a drought is coming to Israel. But he does not communicate the doom without sharing the

source of the message. Elijah's greeting to the king was, "As the Lord, the God of Israel lives...there will be neither dew nor rain in the next few years except at my word." Make no mistake, *the* Lord, *the* God of Israel—that is right, the same nation where Ahab reigned—spoke through Elijah.

Elijah is a biblical hero, a notable figure. He is not more important or significant than others, just more well-known. He was a valiant prophet who delivered messages of opposition to God's people for their participation in idol worship and challenged the kings of Israel for leading God's people astray.

For over 90 years eight different kings reigned over Israel. They each allowed, welcomed, initiated and participated in rampant corruption and horrendous evil. Sadly, it was so prevalent it seemed the norm. Providentially, God was not absent or unaware. Elijah's message was clear. The God of Israel lives unlike Ahab's idols which are manmade and dumb.

Why would God choose a drought as His judgement? King Ahab instituted the worship of Baal, the god of fertility and lord of the rain clouds. Baal is powerless behind the Lord of Creation, the God of Israel.

A special prophet was required for this imminent day of reckoning for God's people. If a job description were posted, the qualifications might be bold, confident, confrontational, assertive, resilient, aggressive, uncompromising, and determined. However, interviews were not necessary; God already chose and commissioned Elijah for the mission. Not much is conveyed about the prophet, but 1 Kings 17:1 does reveal his hometown, Gilead.

An old Negro spiritual highlights Gilead. Spirituals are songs expressing hope and deep faith in God. Africans who were brought to the United States and sold into slavery proved through many tunes that though freedom can be stolen, songs in the heart cannot.

There is a balm in Gilead,
to make the wounded whole,
There is a balm in Gilead,
to heal the sin-sick soul

A few times in the Old Testament the mountainous region is mentioned for its medicinal herbs and spices. Jeremiah 46:11 says, "Go up to Gilead and get balm..." The old spiritual refers to Jesus as the balm of Gilead. A balm is anything that soothes, eases, or heals pain.

God sent Elijah to His sin-sick and rebellious nation. Though it would have been difficult to get a face-to-face meeting with the king, since God ordered Elijah's steps, it happened. God desired His people would return to Him. Covenant would not break. Therefore, He always wooed His people back. But they were stubborn and stiff-necked, so God used serious measures to get their attention.

Elijah delivered news of a drought, but he also made a declaration in front of the king. In the middle of the wake-up call, the prophet makes a powerful statement regarding his relationship with the Lord, the God of Israel, saying, "...whom I serve..." The King James Version translates it, "...before whom I stand..."

King Ahab would recognize the royal connotation. The terminology was a common expression showing service to a monarch. Before Israel's reign of evil, priests were anointed as God's representatives: a conduit between the people and their God. Though Elijah stood before the king, he made it clear whom he served.

Elijah's words were meant to alert the king. The forecast was absolute. The devastating drought would bring a famine. The prophet did not stick around to see if the wake-up call was effective.

KEY POINT: FEAST IN THE FAMINE

1 Kings 17:2 says, "Then the word of the Lord came to Elijah." When reading this account, it is quite easy to skim over this verse and get right to the next, but sometimes we need to pause. In a musical score intentional rests have purpose. Here, a pause gives us time to focus. We can only listen up if we wake up. *The* word of *the* Lord came. Whoa!

Yes, God sent Elijah to forecast a famine, but He is still in direct communication with His man. One of my favorite Bible verses is Jeremiah 15:16. "When your words came, I ate them; they were my joy and my heart's delight, for I bear Your name, O Lord God Almighty." God provided His Word as a direct communication with us. We do not have to wait for His Word to come to us; it already has. Are you feasting?

We seek joy and we search for the desire of our hearts. At times we claim we are in a drought, dwelling in a dry place where God's voice cannot be heard. We are seeking and searching for what has already been supplied. We need a wake-up call! Folks, Jeremiah tells us, we have a feast, no matter the famine! Perhaps we struggle to feast on the Word because we are only willing to wear His name, not bear it.

Followers of Jesus are good at wearing His nametag, but proclaiming His salvation, His holiness, or His character to our friends, family, neighbors, and co-workers is a demand some ignore and avoid.

The Bible is God's Word, not just words. His Word is a feast, not a smorgasbord. When the word of the Lord came to Elijah, it sustained him, filled him, and satisfied him as he left the palace and waited for directions and a plan for provision.

KEY POINT: IN A FAMINE GOD DIRECTS AND PROVIDES

God said, "Leave here, turn eastward, and hide in the Kerith Ravine, east of the Jordan. You will drink from the brook, and I have ordered the ravens to feed you there." (1 Kings 17:3-4)

Elijah's directions were leave, turn, and hide. The drought would be difficult and the famine very hard on the people. For years this nation turned away from God and refused to repent. God's judgement was a drought. His people no longer loved or listened to God, so His discipline included isolation from the rebellious ones He still loved. Therefore, since Elijah was His representative, he must be hidden.

Jehovah Jireh means the Lord will provide. In Genesis 22 Abraham's obedience was tested. God told him to take his son and sacrifice him on an altar. Abraham followed God's direction as his son followed him up Mt. Moriah to the place of sacrifice. On the way Isaac asked his father, "Where is the lamb for the offering?" The father responded, "God himself will provide."

Father and son prepared the altar and Abraham laid Isaac on it. As the father went for the knife, the angel of the Lord cut in, shouted his name, and told him to not lay a hand on the boy. Then Abraham looked up and saw a ram caught by its horns. God provided his offering, and on the prepared altar, Abraham sacrificed it instead of his son. Abraham called that place Jehovah Jireh.

A faithful God expects faithful followers. Droughts come. Hard times happen. Famines occur. Will we trust God to be faithful in the famine? Will we remain tucked in tight to Him and feast on His promises in the drought? God didn't bring the ravine to Elijah. But He gave the directions on where to go. It was his choice to follow. If he obeyed he would receive the promise of God.

1 Kings 17:5 says, "So he did what the Lord had told him. He went...and stayed..." In the previous chapter we saw what happened when David remained. Staying put isn't wrong. What matters is who gave the order. Elijah stayed where God led; David remained out of selfish ambition and pride.

Elijah did not need to wonder or worry about his sustenance because God told him what to expect. He would drink from a brook and ravens would bring his meals. A brook, in a drought. Ravens, his DoorDash delivery mode. Ravens are birds of prey, more apt to take meat than deliver it. But the living and faithful God of Israel kept a private brook flowing and ordered a far-fetched source to fly in and feed Elijah.

1 Kings 17:6 confirms, "The ravens brought him bread and meat in the morning and bread and meat in the evening, and he drank from the brook." God met Elijah's needs with a predetermined schedule. Elijah had nothing, yet he had enough. Through the drought he trusted in God's provision and waited for God's direction.

KEY POINT: DRIED-UP FAITH IS NO GOOD IN A DROUGHT

1 Kings 17:7 says, "Some time later the brook dried up..." Just because the brook dried up doesn't mean God abandoned Elijah. If we feast on the promises of God, we trust He will be with us and carry us through all droughts. Joshua 1:9 promises, God will never leave His children. Psalm 23 assures He is with us through the valley of the shadow of death. Psalm 40:11 guarantees we are always

STAND ready / Ellen Harbin

protected by the Lord's love and truth.

When we face famines it is imperative we take our eyes off the difficulties and hardships and fix them on the Author and Perfecter of our faith. (Hebrews 12:2)

What is your response when a brook dries up? Anxiety? Frustration? Despair? Do you cast blame or question God? God did not dry the brook to discourage Elijah; He dried it up because his prophet was needed elsewhere.

If we lose faith when things dry up, we are not ready to be used for God's purposes. Since He promises His presence, His guidance, and His providential care, we need to remain tucked in tight, wholeheartedly trusting Him. When the living God of Israel dries up the brooks, our first response should be, "I am ready, Lord. Use me in any fight worth fighting for." When we are ready to fight, God speaks. *Then the word of the Lord came to him.* (1 Kings 17:8)

God knew Elijah was ready, so He gave him his marching orders.

"Onward, Christian Soldiers" is an old hymn of the faith. The Reverand Sabine Baring-Gould hastily wrote the hymn for children to sing as they traveled from one village to the next during a festival. This refrain reminds us of what Paul said to Timothy, "Endure hardship with us like a good soldier of Christ Jesus." (2 Timothy 2:3)

Onward, Christian soldiers, marching as to war,
With the cross of Jesus going on before.

When the brook dries up, God moves us on. When brooks dry up, followers of Jesus must march on. When the brook dries up, our faith must not, for God may be calling us to another worthy fight. Elijah's brook dried up; but he remained faithful and was ready for the call of God.

KEY POINT: FERTILE GROUND CAN BE FOUND IN FAMINES

God said, "Go at once to Zarephath...and stay there. I have commanded a widow in that place to supply you with food." (1 Kings 17:9) The ravens are called off, and a widow is now tasked with being the supplier of Elijah's food. His marching orders are to go and stay.

Years ago, I heard the comedian Steven Wright say he named his dog Stay. That way he could say, "Come here, Stay, come here, Stay." God does not fool around. But sometimes we are like the dog. We hear the call of our Master, and we step into obedience, but we stop moving forward as if our name is Stay.

Elijah moved on. 1 Kings 17:10 says, "So he went to Zarephath." The prophet needs her, and she needs him. The verse continues, "When he came to the town gate, a widow was there gathering sticks." There are times on our faith journey when it is obvious the hand of God is at work, but we do not recognize it as such. We are quick to call it a coincidence or an accident or pure luck.

We need our eyes opened! Imagine Elijah walking into town, seeing a woman at the gate dressed in her widow apparel, and he thinks, "Nah, that cannot be her. Surely there is more widows in this town; I will just sit here by the gate and wait." His wait would have ended in death. Hers and his! The consequences are great when we wait to move after God's directive is clear.

"He called to her and asked, 'Would you bring me a little water in a jar so I may have a drink?" (1 Kings 17:10)

Are you crazy? Where have you been: Under a rock? Can you not you see the people all around? We are hungry and thirsty and weary from the effects of the famine. And

you have the audacity to ask me for a drink?
That is not how this went down!

1 Kings 17: 11 says, "As she was going to get it..." A woman on the brink of starvation, who does not know God, showed an act of goodwill and kindness. Elijah recognized her willingness to help and knew she was the one God handpicked and referred him to. The verse goes on, "...he called, 'And bring me, please, a piece of bread.'"

The widow could have objected with several justifiable reasons to not help Elijah. Instead, she honestly responded, "As surely as the Lord your God lives...I don't have any bread—only a handful of flour in a jar and a little oil in a jug. I'm gathering a few sticks to take home and make a meal for myself and my son, that we may eat it—and die." (1 Kings 17:12)

God provided fertile ground in the widow of Zarephath. Her heart was ripe for the Lord. Fertile soil is readied ground. God sent Elijah outside of Israel and into the heart of the land where Baal worship originated.

There are people in our sphere of influence who are ripe for Jesus. They are ready for His salvation and God's amazing grace. People are ready for forgiveness, hope, joy, peace, and unconditional love. Folks are trying to fight for the things worth fighting for, but they are lost in battle. Their hearts are ripe for Jesus. Are you ready to introduce the Hope of Nations, the Prince of Peace, the Savior of the world into their fertile ground?

KEY POINT: THE LAST SUPPER IS THE BEST MEAL

On the day before Good Friday, Jesus was betrayed by one disciple and denied by another, and as He agonized and prayed in the garden, He was ignored by a few more. He was arrested, falsely accused, deserted, blindfolded, spat on, flogged, beaten, and bound over for trial on the next day. But before all that happened, the disciples enjoyed a meal with Jesus. The Lord's Supper, or The Last Supper, is where Jesus taught His disciples about the bread and the cup.

Maundy Thursday is the day before Good Friday; Maundy is for the Latin word, *mandatum*, meaning commandment or mandate. On that same night Jesus washed the feet of His disciples and said, "A new command I give you: Love one another. As I have loved you, so you must love one another." (John 13:34) Jesus taught and modeled how to serve and love one another.

A famished man or woman is empty and needs filling. An empty soul is hungry and thirsty. Praise God, through Jesus, He provided refreshment and fulfillment! Jesus also tells us to eat often and remember Him.

As Holy Communion is served in our church, the pastor says,

"As we prepare to receive communion,
let us remember that on the night He was
betrayed and offered Himself up for us,
Jesus took the bread, gave thanks to the Father,
gave it to His disciples, and said, 'Take and eat.
This is my body, broken for you.
Eat of it in remembrance of me.'
After the supper, He took the cup,
gave thanks to the Father, gave it to His disciples and said,
'Take and drink. This is my blood, the blood of the new
covenant, poured out for you and for the sins of all.'
Let us pray. Holy Spirit transform this ordinary bread and
cup into the symbolic presence of Jesus,
that we may inwardly receive Him anew.
May we be His hands and His feet in the world.

All glory is yours, now and forever. Amen"

The moment right before Jesus enters our life is the last empty moment our soul will ever know. Where Jesus dwells there is no room for emptiness. Therefore, we should *eat the bread and drink the cup often*—to remember how satisfying and fulfilling He is. Holy Communion truly is the best meal!

KEY POINT: LITTLE IS MUCH WHEN GOD IS IN IT

The widow is picking up sticks to prepare her last meal. Before we say she is an empty woman, we must be careful. It is not true. She has a handful of flour and a little oil. Little is much when God is in it.

Elijah knows a little flour in a jar and a little oil in a jug needs to be turned over to God. He says to her, "Don't be afraid. Go home and do as you have said. But first make a small cake of bread for me from what you have and bring it to me, and then make something for yourself and your son." (1 Kings 17:13)

He continued, "For this is what the Lord, the God of Israel says: 'This jar of flour will not be used up and the jug of oil will not run dry until the day the Lord gives rain on the land." (1 Kings 17:14)

In the early 1900s a train broke down in a blizzard. A man named Fred helped rescue the passengers and get them safely to his house. Sometime later one of the passengers, a young lady named Kittie, wrote a thank-you note to Fred. Correspondence continued, and they were later married. Years after, Fred and Kittie attended a church service and met Jesus. Some time after that they became evangelists. Kittie was also a musician and wrote hymns.

One summer a young preacher, named George,

came and stayed with Fred and Kittie. During a church service George got up to sing as Kittie accompanied him on the piano. He struggled to reach the higher notes. Dejected, he sat down vowing never to sing again. Kittie would have none of that. She lowered the key, and George Beverly Shea went on to sing to the glory of God. George became the well-known baritone who sang on Billy Graham's Crusades. The hymn that became the theme of Kittie's life is "Little is Much When God Is in It."

For the jar and jug to be filled, they needed to be emptied.

KEY POINT: TO BE FILLED WE MUST BE EMPTIED

Paradox is purposeful to our faith journey; therefore, this contradiction should have our attention. When God gets invited in, He fills emptiness. This widow had very little, but Elijah encouraged her to use the little she had left to feed him. If you view this as a selfish man making her meet his need, then you are missing the point of the paradox.

God sent the prophet to the widow. Elijah is walking in obedience, not selfishness. Though Elijah had nothing he is content and still followed God. He was filled with faith and full of trust that the one who provided a brook and ravens will continue to sustain and satisfy him throughout the famine.

Surrendering *all* surrenders every little thing over to God's control. For the widow to be satisfied, she needed to turn the remaining oil and flour over to the Lord. In her hands it was her last meal; in God's, it will be her supply.

The widow was told to use what she had left to *first make a small cake*. She had options—ignore the command, negotiate the terms, or walk by faith. When followers of

146

Jesus engage in negotiations with Deity, we are not ready to fight for the things worth fighting for. Doubt, fear, worry, pride, and stubbornness precede negotiations and leave us full of ourselves.

Yes, God could have filled her jar and jug before she returned home. But for her faith to begin or increase, she needed to be emptied. There are times when we ask, plead, and even expect God to fill us, but He is waiting for us to be emptied. We view empty as loss. God uses empty to fill His followers.

To be filled with faith, ready to fight right, followers of Jesus must be emptied.

KEY POINT: IN FAMINES, LIVING WATER FLOWS

The widow was hungry. Her body needed nourishment, but her soul craved righteousness and holiness. We are no different. If we are looking for sustenance in the famine, we will remain famished. If we seek righteousness and holiness, we will be filled. We struggle to stand ready when we are focused on the famine. Holy living should happen in famines. Righteousness is not only for abundant living.

In Matthew 5:6 Jesus teaches His followers, "Blessed are those who hunger and thirst for righteousness, for they will be filled." Famines threaten our stance. When we are hungry for sympathy, thirsty for retaliation, starved for affection, or longing for fulfilment our souls are in a drought, famished due to life's trials and troubles. Indeed, we are hungry and thirsty. Like the woman at the well in John Chapter four, Jesus is our supply of living water. He says whoever drinks the water He gives will never thirst, and it will become a spring welling up. (John 4:14)

Followers of Jesus possess an inner well that will

never run dry. If we walk by faith in the famine, jars of joy and jugs of peace, jars of hope and jugs of strength, and jars of power and jugs of contentment will continuously spring up from the wells of salvation in your soul.

At times God's ways do not make sense, but to fight right we must obey His commands. After Elijah told the widow to first feed him, 1 Kings 17:15 records, "She went away and did as Elijah had told her." And the wells of salvation sprung up. "So there was food every day for Elijah and for the woman and her family." Just as God promised the jar and the jug remained filled.

KEY POINT: MURPHY'S LAW IS NOT GOD'S WORD

If Mr. Murphy was her neighbor, he would have told the widow, "If something can go wrong, it will." We have all heard someone say, "Just when you think it cannot get any worse, it does." The widow of Zarephath was not an Israelite, but the famine in her neighborhood proved she was affected by their disobedience. The idioms are aplenty. *Out of the frying pan and into the fire. I'm up the creek without a paddle. May as well pour gasoline on this fire. The light at the end of this tunnel ended up being an on-coming train.*

If we look at the widow's circumstances, we only see doom and gloom, hardship and pain, and a situation going from bad to worse. 1 Kings 17:17 reveals her son became ill and, "He grew worse and worse, and finally stopped breathing." And just when she was beginning to know Elijah's God. Again, earthly sustenance cannot feed spiritual famines.

"What do you have against me, man of God? Did you come to remind me of my sin and kill my son?" (1 Kings 17:18) Oh, Lord, be Thou our vision! It is imperative we read this with holy eyes and not human understanding. Man-made mercy will have us pointing our finger at Elijah, revved up with angst and spewing, "Yeah, man, what are you, some kind of holier-than-thou seer sent to ruin a widow's life?"

For just a moment step away from her accusation, and first look at her second question. *Did you come to remind me of my sin?* When we recognize our sinful ways, it is good news. We can assume Elijah introduced her to God and explained the famine. Perhaps she thought God was punishing her sin just as He was angry with the Israelites for their actions.

Just because we think it does not make it true. Her son's death is not Elijah's fault. His presence did not kill her son. God does not cause death as a form of punishment. Her sin and her son are not connected, but her son can be affected by her sin.

My youngest two are adopted. The sins of their biological mother affect them. My sin affects them. Blood has nothing to do with it. My impatience, short temper, and reactive parenting have negative effects on my kids. Should they be harmed in an accident or diagnosed with a disease, it would not be from my or birth mom's poor choices. Earth is not heaven. Bad things happen on earth. At times when things are bad, they may get worse—because we live in a broken and sin-filled place.

But God's Word remains. God's Word is true. God's Word sustains. God's Word brings hope. At God's Word the Light of the World entered this dark domain. And on one Friday afternoon, just before the Light of the World died, three hours darkness came over the entire land. (Luke 23:44-45) His death was for our salvation.

In Matthew 16:22 Jesus predicted His own death. "The Son of Man is going to be betrayed into the hands of men. They will kill him, and on the third day he will be raised to life." Remember, the night before He died, Jesus was in the Upper Room encouraging, serving, teaching, and loving His disciples. Today, *Upper Room* is used to name ministries, devotionals, counseling practices, and blogs that encourage, serve, teach, and love people.

"Elijah took her son...carried him to the *upper room* where the prophet was staying and laid him on his bed. Then he cried out to the Lord, 'Oh Lord, my God, have you brought tragedy also upon this widow I am staying with, by causing her son to die?' Then he stretched himself out on the boy three times and cried to the Lord, 'O Lord, my God, let this boy's life return to him!" (1 Kings 17:19-21)

KEY POINT: IF WE ARE HOLDING IT, GOD CANNOT

The widow did not initiate giving her son to Elijah, but neither did she refuse to let go of him. As she questioned the prophet, she released the hold she had on her son. In chapter three we met Hannah who was bogged down by the weight of her burden. Like Hannah, I imagine this widow was feeling buried under the weight of overwhelming loss. Death of her husband, starvation knocking at her door, watching her son become sick, grow worse, and die probably had her despondent and spent, engulfed in emptiness.

We are inundated with messages, opinions, and guidance on how to handle the struggles of life. Commercials, emails, blogs, memes, friends, articles, co-workers, billboards, books, social media posts...the list goes on. When we are empty, we are vulnerable. Emptiness will have us hang on to anything, even lifeless insight and hopeless advice.

Hang in there. Tough it out. Brace yourself. Ride it out. Keep it together. Just hang on.

Jesus hung on His cross, so we don't have to *hang in there*. We need to hang on to Him! But if we are holding on to our last hope, how can we hold on to Jesus? He is not our last hope; remember, He is our Living Hope!

All too often the message of how to manage hardship reduces the power of God's redemption and lessens the significance of His Word. We toss around *This is just my cross to bear* or *It is what it is* without truly comprehending what we are saying.

Disciples of Jesus are called to be cross bearers. Before Jesus said we are to take up our cross, He said we must deny ourselves. When we are broken and empty, claiming *it's just my cross to bear*, we are focused more on the difficulty than on the command of denial. The cross of Jesus precedes redemption. To bear the cross of emptiness our eyes must be fixed on Jesus and His cross; trusting redemption is possible.

It is what it is implies a message of being stuck in emptiness, rather than sending a clarion of hope. It is true some situations may never change, but that does not mean we should remain stuck in emptiness.

Full surrender to the Lord involves denying ourselves, taking up our cross daily, and following Jesus. What we see as empty, God may choose to use as opportunity for witness or redemptive purposes. Jesus walked a road of suffering, bore the weight of His cross, and took the weight of our sin so we could suffer well in emptiness.

As we walk by faith, we will face suffering and emptiness on the journey. Paul's encouragement to Timothy is also for us. In 2 Timothy 4:5, Paul writes, "...endure hardship..." Earlier in the same letter he said, "...join with me in suffering for the gospel..." Too many followers of Jesus get distracted by holding on to worry and fear of future hardships.

If we are still breathing, we will face difficulty with emptiness around the corner. Instead of facing it with worry and fear, stand ready to bear it well.

KEY POINT: GOOD CAN COME FROM EMPTY

In John 20:11-13, portions read, "…Mary stood outside the tomb crying…" Two angels were present, and they asked, "Woman, why are you crying?" Mary responded, "They have taken my Lord away, and I don't know where they have put him." Mary's focus is on the empty tomb.

When we are feeling empty we are no different than Mary—tunnel vision has us weeping over what we think we see and missing the bigger picture. We cannot be ready to fight for the things worth fighting for if we think Jesus is missing simply because we cannot see Him.

We try so hard to live empty-free lives, but God brings good from emptiness. After Mary claimed Jesus was missing, she turned around and saw Jesus standing there, but she did not realize it was Jesus. (John 20:14) Stuck in her emptiness, she thought Jesus was the gardener and politely asked him, if he carried the body away, to please tell her where he was.

Until Jesus has our attention, we will be engrossed by emptiness. But Jesus calls us out and captivates our hearts. When Jesus called Mary by name, she immediately recognized His voice and turned toward Him. Empty is no longer purposeless when Jesus is in it.

The widow was influenced by Elijah's faith, but she was still void of God in her life. So, Elijah went to battle on her behalf. He was ready to fight for this woman's salvation.

1 Kings 17:22-23 says, "The Lord heard Elijah's cry,

and the boy's life returned to him, and he lived. Elijah picked up the child and carried him down...gave him to his mother and said, 'Look, your son is alive'!" The same God who kept the jar and jug filled in a famine showed up in her emptiness.

In 1 Kings 17:24, we learn the purpose for her emptiness. "Then the woman said to Elijah, 'Now I know...that the word of the Lord...is the truth'." There is no greater *empty* than living a Godless life. People in your sphere of influence are void of Jesus. They need you to stand ready to fight on their behalf. Godless living is a fight worth fighting for!

Are you ready to fight right?

PONDER

deeply, carefully, and thoughtfully consider

1. What emptiness are you currently dealing with in your life? Ellen says *a drought from God is a wake-up call*. What is God trying to awaken in you?

2. What do you tend to feast on in the famines of life? What does God provide in the famines?

3. When you receive Holy Communion, do you treat it like a snack or the best meal served? Explain.

PERSUADE
God's Word influences, encourages, and guides

1. Ellen wrote *famines threaten our stance. When we are hungry for sympathy, thirsty for retaliation, starved for affection, or longing for fulfilment, our souls are in a drought, famished due to life's trials and troubles.* How can the words of Jesus from Matthew 5:6 influence us when we are empty?

2. When you are empty how can Psalm 23 encourage
   and guide?

   Who is the Shepherd?

   What does He make you do?

   Where does He lead?

   What does He restore?

   Where does He guide?

   What valley is He present in?

   Should you fear?

   What brings comfort?

   What does He prepare?

   Who is present at the table?

   What does He do?

   Can emptiness be felt?

   What follows you?

   Where does He say we can dwell?

PRACTICAL
applying Biblical Truth to present day

1. Read 1 Kings 17:2-6.

   How did God provide for Elijah in the famine?

   When you are empty, how has God provided for you in miraculous ways?

   What was God's order for Elijah? (vs. 6)

   Describe how you react when God says, "Stay there" during empty times of life.

2. Notice the verb in 2 Timothy 2:3.

What is it? _____

Now read 2 Timothy 2:7.

What directive did the writer give the reader?

_____

_____

Write your reflections/insights.

_____

_____

_____

_____

_____

PERSONAL
inviting Jesus into your current reality

1. One key point said *if we are holding it, God cannot.*

   What does this personally mean to you?

   Believing the promises of God are true, what happens when we release our emptiness to the Lord.

2. Another key point said *good can come from empty.*

   How does the empty tomb attest to this truth?

   Describe how emptiness in your life demonstrates this truth.

7

be ready to fight when
DEFICIENT

"...those who seek the Lord lack no good thing."
Psalm 34:10

I met Clay in October of 2012. Our church invited him to our town for a weekend. He spoke at a men's conference, preached at the morning worship gatherings, and went to the local high school as a motivational speaker for the student body. Clay is a professional bass fisherman. He is funny, upbeat, engaging, motivating, and inspiring.

Clay has a motto *IF I CAN, YOU CAN*. He began fishing at the age of five, competing in tournaments at fifteen. This natural competitive spirit was transferred to his high school's football field. Clay's determination to never quit and dream big motivates many. But his challenge inspires everyone. Clay was born without legs, missing his left arm, and with a partial right arm. My son, Jaylen, was nine when Clay came to our church.

Two years earlier Jaylen and Sukanya had become a part of our family. On October 28, 2012, at the end of Clay's message at our church he invited anyone who wanted God's gift of salvation to raise their hand. Jaylen was standing next to me. My heart soared as his arm shot up. As I write this I called for Jaylen to come to my office. As soon as he entered, I asked, "Hey, J, when did you ask Jesus into your life?"

Without missing a beat and smile on his face, he said, "October 28, 2012 when Clay gave the invitation. I heard him say it in the earlier service but didn't put much thought to it. So when he said it again, I thought, 'Hey, I want some of this,' so, I decided to raise my hand."

Kevin and I are eternally grateful a limited man came to our church and shared his story of how a limitless God can use anyone for the glory of Jesus. We thank God for Clay and his testimony of fortitude and buoyancy. Our son met Jesus because Clay refuses to allow his challenge to keep him from being the hands and feet of Jesus.

KEY POINT: VALIANCY IS NOT ENOUGH FOR TOTAL VICTORY

Valiancy is described as bold courage, bravery, and stoutheartedness. If you were in combat and had boots on the ground, you would want your commander to be a valiant leader:
In 2 Kings 5:1, Naaman is introduced.

- Commander of the army of the king of Aram
- A great man in the sight of the king
- Highly regarded because of a certain victory
- A valiant soldier

In other versions, it is said he was a mighty warrior, a good and brave soldier, a truly great man, and a mighty man of valor. The Hebrew word for valor is *chayil*. Naaman was a force—he is strong, efficient, and capable.

But.

This conjunction changes the trajectory of the narrative. The end of 1 Kings 5:1 says, "He was a valiant soldier, but he had leprosy." That leaves one more bullet point in Naaman's introduction.

- A leper

Naaman had a disease of the skin. It is unknown how far it had spread on his body or what his exact symptoms were. However, since leprosy was considered vile and repulsive, his life was greatly affected.

Valiancy can carry a person far, and it can bring many victories, but it is not enough to win every battle we face or suffer through. Without God, fear threatens courage, bravery changes to timidity, and stout-hearted people turn into cowards.

Jesus is the Victor. Not *a* victor, *the* Victor. He conquered sin and defeated the grave. Without Jesus, we cannot stand ready to fight for the things worth fighting for. Even the mightiest warrior is deficient in some area and needs Jesus!

KEY POINT: DEFICIENCIES SHOULD NOT AFFECT CHARACTER

We have been deceived to believe, and even accept, that character is controlled and altered by troubling conditions. Other people's mistakes and poor choices leave us deficient. Their sin can make us weak, inadequate, and deficient.

No matter. Even though our character can take a hit, it cannot be taken away. Character gets turned over, not snatched. Your character is attached to your conscious, inclinations, and choices, not to another's.

We all have shortcomings and scarcities. We lack tact, self-control, and patience. At times, we are crabby, short-tempered, and rude. Certain circumstances cause us to fall short in conduct, thought, and ability. Situations control our character and leave us with an insufficient supply of fortitude.

We are not ready to fight right if our character does not stand tall. Clay was born with a challenge. Nevertheless, he decided his limitations would not alter his character. Naaman stood tall in character as well, but he was in distress.

Our insufficiencies will affect others, and though they are responsible for how they will respond, we are still held accountable for how we live with shortcomings and throughout scarcity.

In 2 Kings 5:2, Naaman's wife and her servant girl are mentioned. It says, "Now bands from Aram had gone out and had taken captive a young girl from Israel, and she served Naaman's wife." According to 1 Kings 20:34, a peace treaty was established between Israel and the Arameans; however, there were some border skirmishes. It is not clear when this little maid was captured, but it is clear she was taken captive.

This is one of those accounts that makes me mad! It is not right that a young girl was ripped from her home! It is wrong that a band of Arameans recklessly mishandled a child! If we get emotionally caught up in her capture, we will struggle to see God's handiwork in the situation. To fight right today we cannot be held captive by unfair circumstances, unjust situations, or unscrupulous matters from the past.

If we get triggered from a story in God's Word, we must also be careful as we move on. Before we mix or mingle our reality with the young girl's, we need to first focus on the facts.

Fact # 1 Though captured, God protected her.

Of all the places she could have landed, she ends up at the valiant commander's home. Yes, she is in captivity, but she is ultimately nestled safely in the palm of God's hand. (Isaiah 41:10 & 13) And when we are tucked in tight to Him, we can fight for the things worth fighting for. Though this girl has been taken captive, 2 Kings 5:3 reveals facts about her character.

Fact #2 She was bold.
She said to her mistress...

This implies she was not responding to a question, rather she boldly confronted her mistress. Perhaps Naaman's wife respected her staff. Maybe she allowed the maid to freely speak. Still, discussing clothing options, hair styles, and jewelry choice is not the same as boldly confronting a sensitive subject about your mistress's husband, who happens to be the king's commander.

Fact #3 She was hopeful.
"If only...

The Hebrew word directly translates her saying, "Oh, that...!" This young Israelite girl speaks with a firm hope. Her *if only* isn't spoken out of a hope that something can happen; it is more with an assurance that something will happen. There is a difference when hope longs for something versus knowing.

Fact #4 She was respectful.
...my master...

Authority and position should be respected even if the person holding the title is not worthy of respect. We already saw that Naaman respects his position and stands tall in it. Taken from her home, this girl is in a foreign land, and yet she still honors her mistress and the commander in whose home she lives and dwells.

Fact #5 She was faith filled.
...would see the prophet...

This Israelite girl knew about the prophet Elisha. Perhaps she heard how he stood at the bank of the Jordan River, struck the water with Elijah's cloak, and it divided to the right and to the left. (2 Kings 2:14) Maybe she knew of the time he healed the water in a town because it was bad, and the land was unproductive. (2 Kings 2:19-22) It could be she heard about the time he filled a dry valley with water (2 Kings 3:20) or filled a widow's empty jars with oil (2 Kings 4:6). Or, was it when Elisha predicted pregnancy on a barren Shunammite woman, and a year later she had a son. (2 Kings 4:17)

A few years later the son got sick and died. She left his dead body on Elisha's bed in the upper room of her home and fetched the prophet. In bitter distress she told him about her son. They returned to the upper room; Elisha stretched out on the boy and he grew warm, sneezed seven times, and opened his eyes. (2 Kings 4:8-37)

Later, the prophet was in Gilgal where a famine had struck. While in a meeting with a company of prophets, a stew was prepared with herbs from a wild vine. But the prophets refused to eat *the death in the pot*. Elisha put flour in the pot and revived the stew, and it nourished the prophets. (2 Kings 4:41)

Maybe the girl was influenced when she heard about the bread that was multiplied to feed a hundred hungry men at the command of the prophet. (2 Kings 4:44)

We take communion because Jesus said, "Do this, in remembrance of me." We easily forget, especially when we are deficient. Be encouraged to remember the times God showed up and showed off in your life. The memories will embolden our faith through difficulty and fill us when we feel our faith is at a deficit.

Fact # 6 She was aware.
...who is in Samaria!

When our circumstances have us deficient or we are captured by fear, we need to remain focused. As followers of Jesus our eyes must be fixed on Him and our hearts surrendered and trusting in the providence of God. He is never surprised by our limitations. The Lord knows all about the deficiencies that challenge our faith journey. This girl kept her head in the game. Only the Spirit of God can keep us centered on Christ so we can be aware God is at work.

Fact #7 She was convinced.
...He would cure him of his leprosy."

She overflowed with faith, convinced Elisha *would* recover Naaman, not that he *could* possibly cure him. Her word use means that the leprosy would be completely taken away and removed; his skin recovered from the ghastly disease.

Fact # 8 She was selfless.

In her captivity she thought of the deficiency affecting her master. This girl refused to throw a pity party. Some would say she had the right to fall to pieces; it would be expected for her to act out of character. Instead, this captured girl allowed her character to be captivated by God.

KEY POINT: WHEN WE STRUGGLE TO SEE GOD, HE STILL SEES US

The young maid did not doubt God's existence or His providence. But when we are caught in strongholds, or carried away by sin, or chained to doubt, or fastened to fear, God is not tethered or bound by these deficiencies.

One of my favorite movies is *The Count of Monte Cristo*. Falsely accused, Edmond was taken captive and thrown into prison for treason. After years of solitary confinement, an imprisoned priest dug his way to Edmond's cell. The two prisoners formed a friendship. The priest taught Edmond to read and write. He selflessly imparted vast amounts of knowledge to his pupil expecting nothing in return. The younger man learned and took in all the older one taught.

For years, Edmond was angry and desired vindication. He was set on revenge should he ever escape. So, the priest shared wise counsel, "Here is your final lesson. Do not commit the crime for which you now serve the sentence. God said, 'Vengeance is mine.' "

Edmond responded, "I don't believe in God."

The wise priest countered, "It doesn't matter. He

believes in you."

KEY POINT: EVERY STEP OF FAITH GETS US CLOSER TO GOD

According to 2 Kings 5:4-5, it is obvious Naaman's wife went to Naaman with the advice of her young maid. "Naaman went to his master and told him what the girl from Israel had said. 'By all means, go,' the king of Aram replied. 'I will send a letter to the king of Israel.' So Naaman left..." He began walking by faith.

Naaman started out on this journey not really knowing what would happen. He was inspired by a young girl and influenced by a prophet's reputation.

In 2 Kings 5:7 we read something surprising. "As soon as the king of Israel read the letter, he tore his robes and said, 'Am I God? Can I kill and bring back to life? Why does this fellow send someone to me to be cured of his leprosy? See how he is trying to pick a quarrel with me?"

One would think that the king of Israel—the very nation God has a special relationship with—would be excited and ecstatic to receive news of a foreigner looking for God's representative. Instead, the king assumed it was a prelude to an ensuing battle. Steps of doubt and worry do not draw us closer to God.

Do we pursue God, or does He pursue us? Yes, to both. He is a pursuing and initiating God; He is the one who made a way for us to find Him. God came face-to-face with humanity when He sent Jesus to Earth. His Word promises, if we seek Him, we will find Him. God does not engage in some frivolous form of hide-and-seek where He remains out of sight.

2 Kings 5:8-9 witnesses Naaman pressing on. When Elisha heard about how the king responded, the prophet challenged the lack of faith from Israel's leader and sent

word for Naaman to come to his house. Naaman continued to Elisha's door. And once he arrived a courier gave him Elisha's message. "Go, wash yourself seven times in the Jordan, and your flesh will be restored and you will be cleansed." (2 Kings 5:10) Naaman is looking for a cure; God is looking for obedience.

As we walk by faith, God may ask us to do something that does not make sense. His way may seem ludicrous or ridiculous. God was not asking for Naaman's opinion; He was expecting obedience. Every step of faith will move this man closer to God.

KEY POINT: STEPS OF FAITH LEAD TO STEPS OF OBEDIENCE

Naaman's need is not to be freed of leprosy; his need is to be made whole. Naaman does not need clear skin; he needs a cleansed soul. Naaman expected a cure, after all a little girl told him that is what Elisha would do. And it is true—the prophet has a record of mind-blowing miracles, and with God's orders, he could cure leprosy. Though the man of God can speak for God and perform acts of wonder in His Name, Elisha cannot fill the void in Naaman's soul.

And Elisha cannot take Naaman's steps of obedience for him. Therefore, Elisha was not at the door when Naaman knocked. Pride journeyed with Naaman and exploded when his expectations went unmet. 2 Kings 5:11 says, "But Naaman went away angry and said, 'I thought that he would surely come out to me and stand and call on the name of the Lord his God, wave his hand over the spot and cure me of leprosy.'"

Naaman was influenced by what he had heard and was persuaded by a different prescription of how God should cure him. "Are not Abana and Pharpar, the rivers of

Damascus, better than any of the waters of Israel? Couldn't I wash in them and be cleansed?' So he turned and went off in a rage." (2 Kings 5:12) *I thought* and *Couldn't I* prove pride resided in the man.

Naaman went off in a rage, heated with indignation and spewing venom. He thought the waters of Damascus were better than the Jordan River. Neither of the other rivers had the significance of the Jordan. To the Israelites the Jordan represented the passage from slavery and wandering in the dessert to freedom. What stood as a giant obstacle, God swiftly separated and made a way for the people to cross into the Promised Land. Naaman's fury and hot temper may have suited him on the battlefield, but on his faith journey they led him astray.

We do not openly admit it, but there are times we think we know more than God. His way is clear and His path is paved. Obedience follows God every step of the way. But pride has us considering and creating a different plan. As we notice deficient followers taking missteps on their faith journey, we should act.

A few years ago we experienced a difficult time in ministry. Arduous people drained us. We were weakened by mean and rude leaders. Schism, insubordination, and slander were present. We were deficient. There were times I would tell Kevin what I thought we should do and how we should respond. My ideas and plans were good—I was motivated to do the right thing. But doing what I thought was right, did not mean I was ready to fight right.

My husband is a good leader. During that deficient time, he relied on God's ways. I do not recall Kevin ever saying, "I think..." or "Couldn't I..." But I do remember him calling out to God, waiting to hear His voice, and seeking to do as He ordered. Kevin had faith that God would intervene. For four years, as difficult as it was and as deficient as we were, Kevin obediently preached, led, challenged, taught, and faced every day choosing to keep in step with God.

KEY POINT: CONFRONT DEFICIENCY WITH DISCERNMENT

Naaman expected fireworks, the wow factor, an explosive and exciting display of healing. God is not about the performance of a cure. He calls for holiness to be on display in our lives. It is a good thing to pray for God to show up in our lives, but we should also desire He show off—that others see through us the transformation He brings.

Good friends confront brothers and sisters in Christ who have been led astray, lost, or wandering. In 2 Kings 5:13, Naaman's servants confront their master. "My father, if the prophet had told you to do some great thing, would you not have done it? How much more, then, when he tells you, Wash and be cleansed!..."

His servants knew his character, and they knew his motivation for seeking the prophet. Though their master was heated, they discerned how to cool him down. They challenged Naaman with a good question that pointed out his pride. *If he told you to do some great thing, would you not have done it?* They spoke the words, but the Spirt of God seared his heart.

Then he turned around and immediately did as Elisha had said. "So he went down and dipped himself in the Jordan seven times, as the man of God had told him, and his flesh was restored and became clean like that of a young boy." (2 Kings 5:14)

KEY POINT: "THE SPIRIT GIVES LIFE; THE FLESH COUNTS FOR NOTHING"

This declaration from Jesus is found in John 6:63. I

am aware of this verse because my dad, Allen, quotes it often. Each time he mentions it, it is like he is sharing it for the first time. With excitement and awe, this 85-year-old man will say something like, "The Lord teaches me to live this out every day" or "If Allen would step out the way, I could see Jesus was already at work."

Whether a man like my dad who has walked with Jesus for almost sixty years, or Naaman, who after stepping out of the Jordan River began his first day of walking with Lord, each needs a daily reminder that the Spirit gives life.

Naaman's skin is smooth. His flesh is clean. But, according to Jesus, it counts for nothing. Physical healing can lead to spiritual awakening, but since the Spirit gives life, any healed body without a transformation of the soul is still walking dead. Though Naaman's flesh is restored, his heart still needs to be cleansed and his soul satisfied.

And it was! In 2 Kings 5:15, Naaman testifies to this change. "Then Naaman and all his attendants went back to the man of God. He stood before him and said, 'Now I know that there is no God in all the world except in Israel'..." Naaman knew, was confident, and assured God is real. God is present. God changed his life. God is above all other gods. Naaman was physically healed, but more, he was spiritually made alive. God restored his flesh but redeemed his soul.

In 2 Kings 5:18, this man, who before expected a display of godly grandeur, now exhibits the spiritual transformation that took place in his heart. "...may the Lord forgive me for this one thing: When my master enters the temple to bow down to Rimmon and he is leaning on my arm and I bow also—when I bow down in the temple of Rimmon, may the Lord forgive me for this."

That is quite the exhibition of the Spirit giving life! Pride had died and humbleness led. Since his heart bowed in worship before the Lord, his bent knee before Rimmon would only signify an act to assist his king. Naaman was no longer focused on his flesh—and that is a good thing, since it counts for nothing!

Naaman recognized though our knee can bend, our hearts bow. Our hearts were made to worship one thing: the King of kings and the Lord of lords. Jesus declares our flesh counts for nothing because He knows we are deficient. John 6:63 supports that Jesus is full of grace and full of truth:

Grace: *The Spirit gives life*

Truth: *The flesh counts for nothing*

Grace: *The words I speak to you are spirit*

Truth: *And they are life*

KEY POINT: WE ARE DEFICIENT BUT HE IS OMNISCIENT

God knows what we think before we think it. He knows what we will say before it is a thought. He knows our past and future. He knows what tempts us and what will make us stumble and fall.

When we say *I can't take it anymore* it is a true statement. We are not meant to handle deficiencies or struggles or trouble on our own. And we are certainly not capable of managing or maneuvering temptation. 1 Corinthians 10:13 says, "No temptation will seize you except what is common to man, but God is faithful, He will not let you be tempted beyond what you can bear..."

Praise His name! He is omniscient and faithful and knows what our limitations are. The verse goes on to say, "...when you are tempted, he will also provide a way out so you can stand up under it."

Elisha left Naaman with the benediction, "Go in

peace." (2 Kings 5:19) So Naaman left to return home. But before he departed, he tried to thank and pay the prophet with an offering. (2 Kings 5:15) But Elisha would not accept a fee for the work God had done. The prophet profited from God's hand, not man's recompence. But we see in 2 Kings 5:20, Elisha's servant was tempted by the gift.

"Gehazi said to himself, 'Elisha was too easy on Naaman...by not accepting from him what he brought. As surely as the Lord lives, I will run after him and get something from him'..." Gehazi's trouble began when he thought to himself and acted on it. Had he shared his thoughts with his boss and authority, Elisha, 2 Kings 5:21-27 would not be a part of God's Word.

Gehazi was deficient—he lacked good sense, a sound mind, and self-control. He was flawed—he fell to temptation. Satan presented a piece of fruit to Gehazi. It looked pleasing to the eye, so he took it and ate it.

God provided more than one way out for Gehazi. But the servant swallowed the forbidden fruit, and he was temporarily satisfied by his decision. He hurried after Naaman and caught up to the commander. As Gehazi watched the commander get down from his chariot, I wonder if the sight of Naaman's fresh flesh struck Gehazi's conscience. (A way out.)

Naaman inquired, "Is everything alright?" The question gave him time to think about next steps. (A way out.) But Gehazi lied. "My master sent me." (Another bite.) The lies continued. Speaking for Elisha, Gehazi said, "Two young prophets just came...please give them a talent of silver and two sets of clothing." (More bites.)

Naaman believes Gehazi's deception and sent two of his servants ahead with the loot. When Gehazi caught up with the men, he took the stash and hid it. Then he sent the men away and went to Elisha and stood before him as if it was a normal day in the life of a prophet and his servant.

Consider all the ways out God provided. He had opportunity to send Naaman's men back with the stash. He had time to tell Elisha what he had done and make it right again. But he was not ready to do the right thing. Temptation is a deficiency, but God promises we will not be tempted beyond what we can bear. Though God continued to provide ways out for Gehazi, he refused them. Consequently, Gehazi landed deep in sin.

KEY POINT: WHEN WE ARE DEFICIENT, HIS GRACE IS SUFFICIENT

Prior to Paul's proclamation about temptation, in 1 Corinthians 10:12, he warns us, "If you think you are standing firm, be careful you don't fall!" Gehazi thought; but he fell.

At any time all Gehazi needed to do was repent, and God's grace would have forgiven his sin. But Gehazi was controlled by his deficiency. Greed took over. A desire for riches claimed his heart. Selfishness pushed servanthood aside.

It is true: God's grace is sufficient but if our deficiencies determine our stance, we will fall, and He will withhold his pardon.

As Gehazi stood before the man of God, Elisha asked, "Where have you been, Gehazi?"

Gehazi answered, "Your servant didn't go anywhere."

But Elisha responded, "Was not my spirit with you when the man got down from his chariot..." Whoa! God revealed the truth to Elisha. He went on, "Is this the time to take money, or to accept clothes, olive groves, vineyards, flocks, herds, or menservants or maidservants?" Basically, the prophet challenges: *When will enough be enough? When will you be satisfied? Once you opened the door to greed, you fell over the cliff and now you are in deep.* (2 Kings 5:25-26)

Even then, it was not too late for Gehazi to repent. But he did not.

Elisha went on, "Naaman's leprosy will cling to you..." (2 Kings 5:27a) God took the leprosy away from Naaman, but Gehazi's actions brought it back on himself. God takes sin seriously. He knows what it can do to us. He knows how deficient it makes us. He knows how debilitating it is. And that is why He provided the ultimate way out.

The cross of Jesus crosses out sin; His blood cleanses us and makes us whole. Too many followers of Jesus are content to live knowing their sins are forgiven. But there's more! In John 10:10, Jesus says, "I have come that they may have life and have it to the full." The same power that raised Jesus from the dead is the same power available to us in the fullness of God. Only when we are filled with the Holy Spirit can we stand ready to fight.

It is true—Jesus is enough. He is all we need. But He is intertwined in the Trinity. Therefore, we need the creating work of the Father, the redeeming work of the Son, and the sustaining work of the Holy Spirit. As we are filled with the Spirit, we are equipped to stand ready to fight any fight worth fighting for.

Deficiencies exist. Therefore, we need the indwelling and filling of the Holy Spirit. If followers of Jesus feel deficient, perhaps it is because something other than the Holy Spirit is clinging to them.

Naaman's leprosy clung to Gehazi, and that was not all. 2 Kings 5:27 continues, "...and it will cling to your descendants forever." It is not enough to think we are standing firm. We must know we are. God teaches us how to stand firm:

> **Exodus 14:13** *Do not be afraid.* ***Stand firm*** *and you will see the deliverance of the Lord.*

> **Job 11:13-15** *If you devote your heart to him...put away the sin in your hand...allow no evil to dwell...lift your face without shame; you will* ***stand firm*** *and without fear.*

> **Psalm 37:23** *If the Lord delights in a man's way, he makes his* ***steps firm.***

> **Psalm 40:2** *he lifted me out of the slimy pit...set my feet on a rock...and gave me* ***a firm place to stand.***

> **Proverbs 10:25** *...the righteous* ***stand firm*** *forever.*

> **Luke 21:19** *By* ***standing firm*** *you will gain life.*

> **1 Corinthians 16:13** *Be on your guard;* ***stand firm*** *in the faith, be men of courage; be strong.*

> **Colossians 4:12...** *always wrestling in prayer for you, that you may* ***stand firm*** *in all the will of God, mature and fully assured.*

> **2 Thessalonians 2:15** *So then...* ***stand firm,*** *hold to the teachings we passed on to you...*

KEY POINT: WHEN WE ABIDE IN JESUS, SIN CANNOT CLING TO US

2 Kings 5:27 concludes, "Then Gehazi went away

from Elisha's presence and he was leprous, as white as snow." Clinging aftermath can be avoided if we are tucked in tight to Jesus. We cannot stand ready to fight for the things worth fighting for if remnants of sin remain.

Alcoholism runs through my and Kevin's bloodlines. It clings to our family tree, but we have a choice if it will cling to us. We shared this fact with our children, but it is their choice if it clings to them.

Good things can cling as well. What do we pass on to future generations? Do we want to highlight our deficiencies or the sufficiency of Christ?

As long as we are breathing, we will be deficient in some way. But as long as we stand firm on Christ the Solid Rock, abiding in Him, each day filled with the Holy Spirit, we will be ready to fight for the things worth fighting for and to live as Jesus intends.

PONDER

deeply, carefully, and thoughtfully consider

1. What limitations do you have that God can use for His purposes?

2. In John 6:63 Jesus says, *the Spirit gives life, the flesh counts for nothing.*

   What area/areas of your life need the Spirit to give life?

   How are you challenged by this verse?

PERSUADE
God's Word influences, encourages, and guides

1. A key point said *steps of faith lead to steps of obedience*. How do these verses persuade you to a deeper faith in God?

   2 Chronicles 20:20

   Lamentations 3:19-23

   Romans 4:20

   Psalm 89:8

   Psalm 100:5

2. When your limitations leave you disappointed or discouraged, how can the following Scriptures help?

   Jeremiah 9:24

   Nehemiah 9:31

   Deuteronomy 32:4

   Jonah 4:2

PRACTICAL
applying Biblical Truth to present day

1. At times our limitation will not be a physical, mental, or an emotional struggle. Temptation to disobey God will have us deficient. Read 1 Corinthians 10:13. Apply this verse to a temptation you currently struggle with. Explain.

2. We can *think* we are standing firm, but we must *know* we are. How can Job 11:13-15 help us to stand firm?

3. In 2 Kings 5:3 a young girl was captured, yet she still demonstrated godly character. Next to the trait, name someone you know who is influential and encouraging in your life.

Bold_____

Hopeful_____

Respectful_____

Faith-filled_____

Aware_____

Selfless_____

PERSONAL
inviting Jesus into your current reality

1. Ellen said *we are not ready to fight if our character does not stand tall.* No matter the deficiency or limitation, we should be ready to fight right. Where are you deficient in character?

   How can the sufficiency of Christ overcome your deficiency?

8

be ready to fight the PAST

"...do not dwell on the past."
Isaiah 43:18

Everyone has a past. Except God. He is eternal—outside the bounds of time. God sees all of history and the future all together. Our finite minds cannot compute the complexity of eternity, but faith-filled hearts will accept God's infiniteness.

In *STAND* strong, I use the vantage points when driving a vehicle as an analogy for trusting Jesus with our next steps. *The windshield shows us a panoramic view of where we are headed. The rearview allows the driver a snapshot of what is behind.* On our spiritual trek we benefit by looking back. Snapshots through the rearview teach us lessons as we walk by faith.

Isaiah's words tell us not to dwell on the past. Isaiah 43:18 begins, "Forget the former things..." How did the Israelites reconcile the command to forget with the instruction within the Ten Commandments? "Remember that you were slaves in Egypt…" (Deuteronomy 5:15) So, the directive from an Eternal God for His followers is to forget and remember?

It is not surprising we struggle with the past. We try to forget what we do not want to remember. And we remember what we strive to forget.

Motive matters. But where the motive originates matters more.

KEY POINT: MATTERS OF THE HEART MATTER MOST

Are we to forget our past or remember it? The answer is yes to both when the purpose is holy. Context is important. Confusion and chaos reign when followers of Jesus try to forget their past without remembering God can bring good from it. Romans 8:28 reminds us, "And we know that in all things God works for the good of those who love him, who have been called according to his purpose." Do you love God? Then God works for your good.

In and of themselves the horrible and despicable acts done to you and any sin you have committed are not good. But God is good, and He does good, and He promises to bring good to the life of one who is set apart for His purposes.

"Forget the former things…" (Isaiah 43:18) We focus more on *the things* than on the God who has spoken. We will never see the good or the new thing God desires to do in our life if we are only gazing in the rearview mirror.

If our motive is to seek retribution, to understand why significant actions occurred, or to just be heard, then we are controlling the outcome. Will we see some good? Perhaps, but manmade good will not bring lasting contentment, pure joy, or eternal hope.

Forgetting the former things, or said differently, not

allowing the past to falsify or distort perspective, requires a holy heart. We need a shift in our souls to trust God no matter what. We need a resolute commitment to leave the past in God's hands, regulate our life through faith, and look for the new thing God promised He would do. (Isaiah 43:19)

Considering *what if I had never done_____, or if only _____, or I regret not _____, or things would be different if _____* wastes a lot of time, emotional energy and mental space. Remember, the flesh counts for nothing. Regret and remorse are good motivators to moving forward, but a heart set apart for God's purposes is influenced by Him.

Prior to God speaking through Isaiah to His people telling them to forget the former things, He reminded them who He was and what He had done. After He told them to stop dwelling on the past, He spoke of providing a new thing, making a way in the desert, and providing streams in the wasteland. (Isaiah 43:19)

It is okay to remember what God has done, but if we only look through the rearview, we will miss how God paves ways where there seems to be no way. If we keep telling others only what He did for us, we will miss the new things He has planned for us. When we are stuck in the dry, barren desert, thirsting and hungering for God, but trying to draw sustenance from the past, we will miss the streams in the desert our good Father provides. He will never waste a wasteland, but we can miss His mercies.

KEY POINT: *HOWEVERS* CHANGE THINGS

Trending throughout Judges, 1 & 2 Samuel, and 1 & 2 Kings are the depravity and dishonesty of God's people. Noted in an earlier chapter, there was always a remnant of righteousness amidst the corrupt.

Around 930 BC, Israel split into two nations, with Israel to the north and Judah to the south. Almost 300 years later, Josiah is crowned king over the southern nation. Before him, 14 monarchs reigned over Judah. Of them, five were downright evil in the eyes of the Lord and nine did what was right.

However.

*On the other hand. Unfortunately. Yet. While this may be true...*of the nine, five have a however following the statement that mentions their right stance. So-and-so did right in the eyes of the Lord, however. This adverb, or conjunctive adverb, connects two clauses or sentences. If we ignored the *howevers* in 1 Kings 22:43, 2 Kings 12:3, 14:4, 15:4, and 15:35, we would miss a crucial connector. Though it is written that each of the five royals did what was right in the eyes of the Lord, they each left the high places standing—a central location for idol worship.

As we walk our faith journey, if things are still standing that God commands we tear down, we may take steps forward but a *however* is prominently in our rearview. When the past remains present, we will dwell on it. We must properly deal with the past or it will influence us.

When he was eight-years-old Josiah became king of Judah. And he was not the youngest. His ancestor, Joash, or some versions say Jehoash, began his reign at seven. Throughout Josiah's 31-year reign, he did what was right in the eyes of the Lord. 2 Kings 22:2 says, "...he walked in all the ways of...David, not turning aside to the right or to the left."

In the eighteenth year of Josiah's reign, he sent his secretary, Shaphan, to the temple regarding a business matter. He was told to see Hilkiah the high priest. When Hilkiah saw Shaphan, the priest had another pressing subject to share with the secretary.

2 Kings 22:8 says, "Hilkiah the priest said to Shaphan the secretary, 'I have found the Book of the Law in the temple of the Lord.' He gave it to Shaphan who read it."

Shaphan returned to King Josiah; let him know the business venture was concluded and then he informed the king about the missing book. He said, "Hilkiah the priest has given me a book." (2 Kings 22:10)

KEY POINT: RESOLVE IF THE BIBLE IS *A* BOOK OR *THE* BOOK

Normally *a* and *the* are simple words. We gloss over them because they do not require critical explanation or clarification. However, the priest reported that he found *the* Book of the Law. Shaphan informed the king about *a* book the priest had given him. In this case the simple words are powerful.

If your Bible is buried deep on the go-to list, unopened, rarely studied, or neglected, then to you it is just a book. However, if it is sought for wisdom, read for pleasure, studied with zeal, and seen as God communicating to us, then it is accepted as *The* Word of God.

When Hilkiah found the Book of the Law, it was not the Bible. Some believe the priest found the Pentateuch, while others think he found portions of it. Historians differ on opinion. The Pentateuch is what we know as the first five books of the Bible. Either way, it impacted and influenced the king.

2 Kings 22:11says, "When the king heard the words of the Book of the Law, he tore his robes." The King James Version says he rent his clothes. For 18 years King Josiah had the past sins of Judah on his mind. He was careful and intentional to walk with the Lord. Over those years he was grieved with people living corrupt and the blatant disregard

for their nation's heritage.

Josiah modeled how to live right. And he was ready to fight right for his nation to return to God. But their past was in the way. The king's integrity was on display, and it was good. But it was not enough to fight the bondage to their past.

KEY POINT: REND YOUR HEART, NOT YOUR ROBE

We cannot interpret the Word of God without the Spirit of God revealing it to us. The Book of the Law was God's communication in Josiah's day. On their own the words could influence Josiah, but they could not speak directly to his heart. When the king heard the words, it is because God's Spirit wrote on his heart and opened his understanding.

The remodeling and renovating of the temple were primary on Josiah's mind. But God readied Josiah to receive His word and spoke to his heart. And a renovation of a heart began.

Josiah's father and grandfather did evil in God's sight. Josiah was fully aware of their sinful ways. The high places erected in Judah long before he reigned were scattered about and standing tall. Josiah was not blind; he constantly noticed the representation of the past. Head knowledge is awareness. But a revelation of the heart makes us responsive.

A torn robe signified intense grief. Josiah was torn up about the despicable things his forefathers did. Then God convicted his heart about the things standing in the way of Judah being restored back to God. The temple required renovation, but the people needed revival and restoration.

In 2 Kings 22:12, Josiah formed a committee of five,

charged to pursue revival. He gave orders to his task force. When pieces of our past get in the way of wholehearted devotion to Jesus, we too need revival.

A Revival Strategy

Step #1 - Go and Inquire of the Lord

2 Kings 22:13 says, "Go and inquire of the Lord..." When we know God has revealed a need for change in our life, He is the first option for seeking wisdom and guidance. In times of need we have many choices who we will turn to for advice.

Recently I was talking with a woman who is struggling and needs a soul revival. During one of our conversations I got the impression she was sharing her story with others. Come to find out, many others. I asked her if all the people she unloads on are Christians. She answered, "Most are."

Then I asked, "How many different pieces of advice are you getting?"

"Many," she replied.

"Are they helpful?" I asked.

"Well, I am still spinning out of control. So, no." She cried and I silently inquired of the Lord, "Oh, Jesus, be my wisdom and my guide. Holy Spirit, fill me and filter my words."

Step #2 - Go to the Book

The five men were to inquire of the Lord, "...about what is written in this book that has been found." (2 Kings 22:13) Josiah knew the Book had life-changing value. He knew God was speaking through it. He knew what the Lord had to say was pertinent to the revival of his nation. Josiah was expectant and confident that his next steps toward wholeness could be found in The Book.

Step #3 - Recognize God's anger

Josiah continued the order, "Great is the Lord's anger that burns against us..." (2 Kings 22:13)

God hates sin. And so should we. What classifies as sin often seems up for debate. We spend more time disputing issues instead of defining sin. John Wesley defines sin as *unbelief*. Billy Graham says *we sin by thinking evil, speaking evil, acting evil or omitting good*. My husband says, "Saying no to God, whether aware or unaware is sin." Adam and Eve did not believe God's word—they took Satan at his word.

When we doubt, question, alter, or refuse God's Word, we sin. For generations, Judah was separated from God because of sin. They doubted God, questioned God, altered His Word, and refused to follow His ways. And God's anger burned.

Step #4 - Know what precedes God's anger

After Josiah recognized God's anger, he mentioned what came first. "...because our fathers have not obeyed the words of this book..." (2 Kings 22:13) To be clear, God loves people, but hates sin. Too many followers of Jesus get this twisted in their psyche. Remember the flesh counts for nothing, so the Holy Spirit overrides the psyche. Being filled with the Spirit changes our thought patterns.

God cannot hate His children even though they disregarded their covenant with Him and stopped following His ways. Disobedience preceded God's anger against

Judah. This fresh revelation of his nation's sin came to Josiah. No longer did he just think the past things were bad; he now knew their sinful past was done against God. Josiah simultaneously felt the weight of God's wrath and knew the depth of His great love and was compelled to fight for righteousness to reign once again.

Step #5 - Obedience is absolute

Josiah concluded, "...they have not acted in accordance with all that is written there concerning us." (2 Kings 22:13) Interesting, the king uses *they* when referring to what was done in the past. However, his use of *us* implies accountability in the present tense. God gave The Book to their ancestors, but it was intended for all future generations to follow.

The Bible expounds on the sinful choices of people. Throughout Scripture we read accounts of brutality, mischief, abuse, murder, immorality—vile, corrupt and evil ways of life. But we can also read when God's people faltered and failed. Their stories are for our benefit and advantage.

Throughout the Bible sin is rampant, but God's grace is pervasive; disobedience is extensive, but God's forgiveness is available; transgression is widespread, but God so loved the world He gave His Son, that whoever believes shall not perish but have eternal life. (John 3:16)

God expects that we fully obey His commands. Not because He's a taskmaster; rather, our hearts are designed to welcome and live for one Master. Judah's trouble began and carried throughout generations when they waivered on commitment and devotion.

KEY POINT: GOD READIES A FAITHFUL FOLLOWER

Josiah's band of leaders followed their orders. Exhilarated by Josiah's expectation and inspired by his revelation they seem to know exactly where to go. "Hilkiah, Ahikam, Acbor, Shaphan, and Asiah went to speak to...Huldah..." [2 Kings 22:14]

Step #6 - Find the one who will speak the truth

When the past wrongly invades the present, we need to be ready to fight right. When the past holds us captive in the present, it is time to fight right. When fighting the power of our past, we need a wise strategist. We need someone who lives right and fights right. When others look to culture instead of Christ, when they accuse you of being narrowminded when you want to remain on God's straight path, when friends ridicule and desert, you need to call on a faithful follower of Jesus.

We may think we have to do it alone because no one will understand, or we do not want to be a bother. Maybe we are embarrassed, or shy, or feel silly, or think we are unworthy to invite another into our fight. Rest assured, God handpicks and assigns faithful warriors for us.

Years ago, I was in a battle over my past. Decisions and choices I had made crept into my mind, invaded my dreams, and affected my behavior. *How can this be happening? I gave that to the Lord.* The questions and doubts came, but the answers and peace evaded me. I told no one.

Until one day I was sitting in a Bible Study with my Bible opened on my lap, and God broke through the uncertainty and spoke truth to my wounded heart. His words were not audible, but they were intense on my heart. "Ellen, are you willing to be broken for Me?"

My inward response surprised me. "Of course, I

am." I thought broken was what I had already experienced, so I assumed that marked the first day of a new way of living for me. And I was right, but I was so wrong on what a *new way* meant. I interpreted this newness as happy, and trouble-free, and painless.

Two days later, trouble erupted in my life. I was discontent, fighting with my husband, angry with my kids, and wanting to be alone. I escaped our tiny townhouse and went to the laundry facility. (Clearly, I was not in practice of running away from home.) God met me in that small space.

When I returned home I called my friend, and mentor, Bette. For the first time I shared my past secrets with someone. I told her everything. God had prepared her for our conversation. She listened well, corrected my thinking, prayed over me, and shared truth from God's Word.

To fight right against the power of my past, areas in my life needed to be broken. And I had given Him permission to do it. In His mercy and grace, He called on Bette to be the one to fight alongside me in my battle to be freed from the chains of my past.

KEY POINT: BEING READY IS AVAILABLE AND ACCESSIBLE

Bette was ready when God moved me to call her. Huldah was ready to fight on behalf of Judah when Josiah's taskforce came calling. 2 Kings 22:14 tells us a bit about Huldah. "...(they) went to speak to the prophetess... who was the wife of Shallum...keeper of the wardrobe. She lived in Jerusalem, in the Second District."

- She was a prophetess.

Huldah spoke for God. It was an assignment from

the Lord. At times He leads us to do hard things, to be counter-cultural, or unpopular. Like Deborah, Huldah was equipped to handle disputes, share wisdom, correct misguided belief, and admonish disobedience to God's ways. But unlike Deborah who was positioned under the palm named for her, though Huldah did not have a prophetess booth, her reputation was solid, and she was available and accessible to the king's men.

- She was a wife.

This does not mean that one must be a wife to be used by God or to apply the key point to their life. It is simply informative, yet helpful. Her husband was the keeper of the king's wardrobe. He had the honorable position. It is quite possible as the royal advisors approached their door, the people began gossiping. *Uh-oh, I wonder what happened. They must have bribed the king for him to consult her. I think she's finally being told to shut-up. After all we can serve what and whom we want, and anyway, Huldah has never approved of the idols in the temple.* People talk—they spew, they conjecture, and they are wrong. Their talk should never impede our availability.

- She was a hometown girl.

God called Huldah to a worthy fight against the sin of her people's past. She was not looking for popularity she was listening to the voice of truth. Righteousness seeks God's favor, popularity gets approval. God calls us to be available and accessible to our people, not approved by them.

KEY POINT: BE READY TO SPEAK UP

God does not call us to offer a piece of our mind; He calls us to be agents of peace and couriers of truth. If we are to speak up for Him, we must use His words, not our opinions or thoughts. Huldah was ready to speak when the royal committee arrived. (2 Kings 22:15-20)

"...This is what the Lord, the God of Israel says..."

She did not use customary speech. There was no royal greeting or should-it-please-the-king jabber. The five men would have no reason to be confused on who the message was from.

"...Tell the man who sent you to me..."

That will snap royal advisors to attention. Tell *the man*? Doesn't she mean *the king* or *your honorable majesty*? Josiah is their king, but God is his ruler, and this is His discourse.

"This is what the Lord says: I am going to bring disaster on this place and its people, according to everything written in the book the king of Judah has read..."

This is a common place in Scripture where some stop reading and begin shaking their head. Unbelief is not the issue; disbelief has them incredulous. If this is you, listen up! On our way to revival, God reveals past sin that stands in the way of our relationship with Him. He reveals it so we will repent of it, and then He will revive our souls. We avoid God's judgment because we just want to see His goodness.

What if we saw His judgment as good? Perhaps we have our gaze turned one way—on ourselves. Josiah is not seeking God's truth only for himself. His people are on his mind. Fighting the past fights for the future of our people. Our kids need to know the struggles and problems of previous generations. If we tell them for gossip sake, there is no redemptive value. But if we divulge for the sake of righteousness, redemption and revival will come.

A look through the rearview reveals the reputations of Josiah's father, grandfather, and great-grandfather. Hezekiah was his great-grandfather. Portions of 2 Kings 18:3-7 say, "He did what was right in the eyes of the Lord...he removed the high places, smashed the sacred stones and cut down the Asherah poles...Hezekiah trusted in the Lord, the God of Israel...he held fast to the Lord and did not cease to follow him; he kept the commands the Lord had given Moses...and the Lord was with him... "

Manasseh was his grandfather. Segments of 2 Kings 21:2-6 show how this king differed from his father. "He did evil in the eyes of the Lord, following the detestable practices of (other) nations...he rebuilt the high places his father destroyed...erected altars to Baal and made Asherah poles...he bowed down to the starry hosts...he sacrificed his own son in the fire...practiced sorcery and divination and consulted mediums and spiritists. He did much evil in the eyes of the Lord, provoking him to anger."

Amon was Josiah's father. 2 Kings 21:20-22 says, "He did evil in the eyes of the Lord, as his father Manasseh had done. He walked in all the ways of his father; he worshiped the idols his father had worshiped and bowed down to them. He forsook the Lord, the God of his fathers, and did not walk in the way of the Lord."

Josiah knew a good God was in control and trusted His ways. The sinful and disobedient people of Judah were already living in hellish conditions and participating in evil practices. Their doom was sure! Judgement from a good

God saves lives.

"...Because they have forsaken me and burned incense to other gods and provoked me to anger by all the idols their hands have made, my anger will burn against this place and will not be quenched.'..." (2 Kings 22:17) If our hearts burn for anything other than God, it leads to destruction and death. A soul on fire for Jesus will not be quenched. A heart passionately pursuing God's ways, worshiping His Son, and filled with the Holy Spirit will burn bright for His glory.

KEY POINT: A RESPONSIVE HEART MAKES US READY TO FIGHT

Huldah's next words were still God's but personalized to Josiah. "Tell the king of Judah, who sent you to inquire of the Lord, 'This is what the Lord, the God of Israel, says concerning the words you heard: Because your heart was responsive and you humbled yourself before the Lord when you heard what I have spoken against this place and its people, that they would become accursed and laid waste, and because you tore your robes and wept in my presence, I have heard you...therefore, I will gather you to your fathers, and you will be buried in peace. Your eyes will not see all the disaster I am going to bring on this place.'..." (2 Kings 22:18-20)

Earlier God spoke to *the man*. Now in this passage God speaks to the position he holds as *the king of Judah*. At times, allocating title or characterizing position is required, even necessary.

My husband is my pastor, and currently, he is also my boss. Just today, I needed to inform my boss on a potential issue and ask my pastor for his insight on a different matter, yet I also wanted to have lunch with my husband. So, I texted my husband and asked if he was available for lunch, then I sent an email to my boss/pastor asking for a moment of his time.

Kevin received the positioning as I intended. He responded to the text with *I'd love to, Babe*. And to the email he replied, *is this a topic we can discuss during lunch or does this require an appointment?* To others, this seems trivial. Frankly, we do not care. We know the importance of clarifying the title or position. Our marriage must be protected and our jobs, respected.

God was protecting the covenant relationship He had with Josiah and He respected the position the man had as king. To the man, He spoke about the upcoming disaster and what caused His righteous anger. To the king the Lord talked about:

- a responsive heart
  because your heart was responsive

- a heart of worship
  humbled yourself before the Lord

- a contrite heart
  because you tore your robes and wept

King Josiah was ready for revival. He was ready to fight the power of the past and the sins of the people. Yes, God saves us from the penalty of sin. And He saves us from the power of sin. But as long as we are breathing oxygen, we are still in the presence of sin.

A responsive heart is also ready to receive the consequences from the past. Bette helped me apply this truth to my life. Like Josiah, I had responded with remorse and regret over my choices. I repented of them. But I was misguided regarding the consequences—I categorized them as sin. I was in need of revival! If we only believe a responsive heart says *I'm sorry, please forgive me* then we aren't wholly responding to the Lord.

We expect God to disassociate His judgement from His character about fighting the past. A heart of worship and contrition are not separate from the initial response. They are a whole package. We try so hard to ignore, run away from, disguise, rename, and hate the consequences, when God allows them for our growth and for the good of others. If our consequences are used for the salvation of others, then we should never pray them away.

KEY POINT: IN THE FAMILY OF GOD THERE ARE NO GRANDCHILDREN

To be clear all people are not children of God. Only those who call Him Father because they know His Son, love His Son, and receive His Son as Savior are called His children. Jesus has everything to do with becoming a child of God. Christian parents are responsible to introduce their child to Jesus. All Christians are to model God's love, His grace, His forgiveness, His discipline, and His character.

Before we see the revival that Josiah brought to Judah, we need to meet his son that followed him as king. 2 Kings 23:31-32 introduces, "Jehoahaz was twenty-three years old when he became king, and he reigned in Jerusalem three months...He did evil in the eyes of the Lord..." I read that, and loudly proclaimed, *you have got to be kidding me!* That's Josiah's kid! What in the world! To God, before he is Josiah's son, he is a man who has the same choice his father had—follow God or not.

Hey parents, listen up! You cannot carry your kids into heaven. God does not have grandkids.

KEY POINT: REVIVAL BRINGS RENEWAL

The last sentence of 2 Kings 22 says, "So they took her answer back to the king." Then 2 Kings 23 begins with King Josiah's response to Huldah's prophetic message. In the first two verses, it tells how Josiah called all the elders, the men of Judah, the people of Jerusalem, the priests and the prophets—all the people from the least to the greatest. Then the king read all the words from the Book which had been found.

The man has just been told about his death, and he continues to lead as a good king should. He is not seeking alone time, nor is he making plans on handing the throne over to his son. The king has the preservation of his kingdom on his mind. According to the prophetess Judah's desolation is for sure, but Josiah has renewal on his mind because revival is in his heart.

In 2 Kings 23:3 King Josiah led by example. "The king stood by the pillar and renewed the covenant in the presence of the Lord—to follow the Lord and keep his commands, regulations and decrees with all his heart and all his soul, thus confirming the words of the covenant written in this book. Then all the people pledged themselves to the covenant."

In Joel 2:12-13 the prophet says, "Even now...return to me with all your heart...Rend your heart and not your garments. Return to the Lord your God..." When we have walked away from the Lord or refused to follow His ways, He calls us back. His beckoning comes before our retuning.

Revival comes to those who wholeheartedly return. For those who rend their hearts, renewal follows. King Josiah renewed the covenant. Literally, he cut a covenant which meant it was inaugurated and valid.

He cuts to the chase and does not cast blame on his

ancestors. A proper look through the rearview window had him operating with a broader scope—he recognized the current reality and accepted God's judgement on Judah. Therefore, Josiah set the trajectory of his nation in the right direction. Josiah returned to the Lord. Revival came to his heart, and he renewed his covenant with the Lord.

KEY POINT: REMOVE WHAT IS IN THE WAY OF YOUR RELATIONSHIP WITH GOD

I cannot change my past, but I can change how it affects me. On our own we do not have the power to forget the past. However, the Holy Spirit is willing and available to empower us to rise above, press on, and fight for the things worth fighting for.

We expend a great amount of emotional grit, mental stamina, and spiritual weariness trying to remove the past when God commands us to remove what is in the way of our relationship with Him. Truth is, the past is not in our way.

For some, rage is in the way. For others, revenge. High places of pride—*I think I am handling this quite well, thank you very much*—and envy—*she experienced the same thing as me, why is her life better than mine*. These high places need to be demolished.

Shrines of *you have no idea what I have had to deal with* block our view of Jesus and must be tore down. Manmade altars of self-pity, woe-is-me, why me, and it-is-what-it-is have altered our mindset. Romans 12:2 says transformation comes when our minds are renewed. Therefore, the altar that worships me, myself, and I—in attitude, behavior, and expectation, must be desecrated.

Are you ready to be freed from the past? Freed from the chains of bitterness, the bonds of unforgiveness, the lie of *it is what it is*, the deception that says *shame and guilt are just a part of life*? Remember Jesus came that we may have life to the fullest. Chains, bonds, lies, and deception keep us from abundant living. The power of the Holy Spirit breaks chains, burns bonds, covers lies, and slaughters deception.

In Acts 9:4, a man named Saul was walking along the road to Damascus when suddenly a light flashed around him. Jesus spoke and Saul responded by falling to the ground. He asked, "Who are you?" The voice answered, "I am Jesus...now get up and go..." Saul met Jesus. As he began to obey, he opened his eyes, but he could see nothing. Yet he still followed Jesus.

Acts 9:12-13 tells how a few days later he was "...filled with the Holy Spirit and immediately something like scales fell from his eyes and he could see again. He got up...and he regained his strength."

Being filled with the Holy Spirit happened after Saul met Jesus. Renewed vision and regained strength came after he was filled with the Holy Spirit. Josiah did not have this option since the Holy Spirit was not available to people until Pentecost which occurred after the death, resurrection, and ascension of Jesus.

However, the Spirit of God authorized and allowed Josiah to remove what was in the way of his covenant relationship with the Lord. Without the Spirit of God, the high places, shrines, altars, chains, bonds, lies, and deception could not be removed.

As we scan through 2 Kings 23:1-25, we can see all the removal actions of Josiah. If it was in the way of Judah's relationship with God, it was removed (vs. 4, 11, 12, 16, 19), burned down (vs. 4, 6, 11, 15), did away with (vs. 5), tore down (vs. 7), desecrated (vs. 8, 10, 13), broke down (vs. 8,), pulled down (vs. 12), smashed, cut down, covered (vs. 14), demolished (vs. 15), slaughtered (vs. 20), and gotten rid of (vs. 24).

Josiah is our example of how we fight the past. 2 Kings 23:25 says, "...(Josiah) turned to the Lord as he did—with all his heart and with all his soul and with all his strength..."

We are not ready to fight if we are not filled with the Spirit. Followers of Jesus who desire to be ready to fight for the things worth fighting for requires, like Saul, being filled with the Holy Spirit. To be ready to stand firm in our faith, God directs, instructs, and commands we turn to Jesus with all our heart, with all our soul, and with all our strength.

PONDER
deeply, carefully, and thoughtfully consider

1. Is your past a hindrance for spiritual growth? Explain.

2. King Josiah knew that the former things were in the way of his people's relationship with God and they needed to be removed. In 2 Kings 23 we read of the removal actions of Josiah.

   What needs to be removed from your life?   What removal action will you use?

   _____   _____

   _____   _____

   _____   _____

   _____   _____

PERSUADE
God's Word influences, encourages, and guides

1. Read Isaiah 43:18-21. When you are bothered or haunted by your past, how can this passage encourage you?

2. In 2 Kings 22:8, Hilkiah reports he found *the* Book of the Law. In 2 Kings 22:10, Shaphan informed the king that Hilkiah found *a* book.

   To you, is the Bible *a* book or is it *the* Word of God?

   How do these Scriptures influence how you view the Bible?

   Psalm 119:89

   Psalm 119:105

   2 Timothy 3:16

   Hebrews 4:12

3. Based on 2 Kings 22:18-20 King Josiah was ready to fight. Unscramble the word, fill in the blank, and explain how each are necessary for revival

He had a _____ heart

p e v r e s s i o n

He had a _____ of worship

a t h r e

He had a _____ heart

t e o t n c i r

PRACTICAL
applying Biblical Truth to present day

1. According to 2 Kings 22:2, Josiah lived right.

   How did he live right?

   How can you apply this principle to your life today?

2. Huldah had a harsh message for Josiah from God.

   How did Josiah respond? (2 Kings 23:3)

   Write his renewal plan.

   Write out your renewal plan.

PERSONAL

inviting Jesus into your current reality

1. Read Joel 2:12-13. What does it mean to you to rend your heart?

2. Who do you have in your life who will speak the truth to you?

   Why did you choose them?

   What, if anything regarding your past, do you need to divulge so you can be ready to fight right?

CONTACT INFORMATION

Send an email to elllen@ellenharbin.com

- if you would like to keep updated on Ellen's speaking and writing

- if you are interested in having Ellen speak at your women's retreat, conference, or event

- if you would like to have Ellen as a guest (via SKYPE, Google Hangouts, or a phone call) at your *STAND ready* Bible Study

- if you'd like to discuss hosting a STAND women's conference at your church or in your community

Find Ellen at ellenharbin.com

Follow Ellen on:

Facebook: facebook.com/ellenmharbin

Instagram: instagram.com/ellenharbin

ABOUT THE AUTHOR

Ellen Harbin is a gifted Bible teacher and conference speaker, creatively applying the truth of God's Word to everyday life. Ellen is the founder and visionary of the "STAND women's conference" based in southeast Michigan. Through her teaching you will be encouraged to grow, challenged to change, and influenced to live as Jesus intends.

Ellen is married to Kevin and lives in Michigan. They have four married children, two teenagers, and one grandchild. Ellen loves deep conversations, laughing hard, spontaneous fun, sunrises, and quality time with friends.

Ellen says being a follower of Jesus is unquestionably the best decision she has ever made.

Made in the USA
Monee, IL
19 May 2021